Departures and Arrivals

One of Canada's most acclaimed writers, Carol Shields is the recipient of the Pulitzer Prize for literature, the National Book Critics Circle Award, the Arthur Ellis Crime Novel Award, the Canadian Authors Association Award for Best Novel, the Governor General's Award for Fiction, and many more. Her numerous novels, two collections of short stories, three volumes of poetry, and five plays (including *Thirteen Hands* and *Fashion, Power, Guilt*, both published by Blizzard), have been among North America's best-received writing in recent years. Some of her works are set in Winnipeg, where she lives and where she teaches at the University of Manitoba. *Departures and Arrivals* is her first published play and was last produced in Kobe, Japan.

DEPARTURES & ARRIVALS

Carol Shields

Blizzard Publishing
Winnipeg • Buffalo

First published 1990 by Blizzard Publishing Inc.
73 Furby Street, Winnipeg, Canada R3C 2A2
Reprinted 1993, 1997.

Distributed in the United States by General Distribution Services,
85 River Rock Dr., Unit 202, Buffalo, NY 14207-2170.

Cover by Terry Gallagher, Winnipeg.
Printed for Blizzard Publishing in Canada by Kromar.

Blizzard Publishing gratefully acknowledges the support of the
Manitoba Arts Council and the Canada Council to its publishing program.

Cataloguing in Publication Data

Shields, Carol, 1935–
   Departures and arrivals
   A play.
   ISBN 0-921368-13-5
I. Title.
PS8587.H544D46 1990 C812'.54 C90-097132-0
PR9199.3.S454D46 1990

Production Credits

Departures and Arrivals was workshopped in draft form in 1983 by the Manitoba Association of Playwrights, directed by Bob White, and first produced in 1984 by The Black Hole Theatre at the University of Manitoba, under the general direction of Chris Johnson, with music by Rob Matheson.

Playwright's Note

The play's structure (twenty-two vignettes) is intended to be open so that separate scenes can be omitted to meet time requirements or re-shuffled to suit the demands of an individual director. The scenes are not distinguished in the text, and directors should feel free to adjust the stage directions and transitions between scenes.

The play is designed so that the many parts can be taken by six actors, three men and three women. Costumes are minimal: a hat, a coat, a prop, and so forth. In addition to the six actors, there is an off-stage Public Address (PA) voice which announces flights and provides connections. (In the Black Hole production, this "voice" was an on-stage presence, an actor/musician who also provided musical accompaniment on an electric piano.)

Although the play is not a musical, some form of musical connection (organ, piano, flute, etc.) helps to join the separate scenes.

It is my hope that all the elements of the play will contribute both to a cyclical sense of arrival and departure, and to the human appreciation of the public place—be it airport, train station, or city street—as a venue for the theatrical sense that enlarges ordinary lives. It is also my hope that the play will realize a fusion of the real and the surreal, the naturalistic and the fantastic. This is a comedy with edges.

—Carol Shields,
June 1990

5

Act One

(Scene: the foyer of an airport. There are two stairways side by side at centre stage, one marked "Departures," the other "Arrivals." To one side is a revolving platform for suitcases with a chute to feed it. At the other side is an automatically opening door to the outside. The foyer has a bench or two, a public telephone, and one or two information desks. Other furniture or equipment is brought on as needed.

At rise, a single piece of luggage, a small exotic vanity case of green, pink and silver, goes around on the platform several times. An airport CLEANER walks across the stage with a big push-broom; he turns and recrosses. PA announcements give flight arrival and departure times. Strobe lighting on stage. People—WOMAN IN SILK DRESS, MIDDLE-AGED MAN, YOUNG MAN, ELDERLY WOMAN, WOMAN OF THIRTY, MAN IN BROWN SUIT, WOMAN IN BROWN SUIT, MAN IN SWEATER, WOMAN WITH SHAWL, and MAN WITH BRIEFCASE—enter from various corners carrying suitcases, wheeling trunks, pushing luggage carts, etc. The music, organ or electric piano, and strobe lights stop; spotlight on one person while others freeze.)

WOMAN IN SILK DRESS: *(Addressing the audience.)* I'm off to London. London, England, that is. I always go to London at this time of year. When I'm in London I always stay at the St. Irmine's, and when I'm at the St. Irmine's, I always have kippers for breakfast the first morning. But I never have a sense of *déjà vu*. Or maybe I have, but I don't know it.

(The strobe lights come on again; people continue to move, then freeze when the lights and music stop.)

MIDDLE-AGED MAN: I'm in sales. Computers. Plastics. About six point eight percent of my life is spent airborne. Does that amaze you? Does that give you pause?

(Lights, music, people moving.)

6

YOUNG MAN: *(Dabbing his eyes.)* I don't want to leave. Not really, not wholeheartedly. This wasn't my idea, this move. But what can I do? On the other hand, I didn't want to come, either.

(Lights, music, people moving.)

ELDERLY WOMAN: Who knows what's going to happen when you get into an airplane. This may be my last scene of reality—that ashtray over there full of butts, that PA voice all stuffed with smiles. Who really knows?

(Lights, music, people moving.)

WOMAN OF THIRTY: I wonder, do I look different? I mean, inside I'm the same person, but, well, not the same person. I mean, does it show? Is he going to ... guess? Does he have the sensitivity to guess? So okay, I've let him down in a sense, but in another sense I've reached out. Oh, hell, if he notices I'll just say I'm coming down with the flu or something.

(Lights, music, people moving.)

MAN IN BROWN SUIT: I'll miss you terribly.

WOMAN IN BROWN SUIT: Me too.

MAN IN BROWN SUIT: It's never easy. Saying goodbye.

WOMAN IN BROWN SUIT: Agreed.

MAN IN BROWN SUIT: It's pain. Anguish.

WOMAN IN BROWN SUIT: Right.

MAN IN BROWN SUIT: Until tomorrow then.

WOMAN IN BROWN SUIT: Tomorrow.

(Lights, music, people moving.)

MAN IN SWEATER: I'm off to Omaha. Spelled O-m-a-h-a. Change planes at Minneapolis. Why Omaha? A good question. Because it's somewhere else, that's why. It's not here.

(Lights, music, people moving.)

MIDDLE-AGED MAN: Wonder if she'll notice I've been working out. Six months of weights, a mile before breakfast, she'd better notice. All this new muscle tissue. I mean, if she doesn't notice, she's gotta be blind or something.

(Lights, music, people moving.)

WOMAN WITH SHAWL: This happens to be my fifth Club Med holiday. Yippee. That first time in Peru, my girlfriend and I, we stayed in our room all night and cried. But later? We really got into it. In a way. You know?

(Lights, music, people moving.)

MAN WITH BRIEFCASE: I'm an MP. So okay, that's a dirty word these days. But take a look at this ticket. Tourist class. Get a load of that. Register that. Re-member that. Think about that.

(Lights, music, people moving.)

YOUNG WOMAN: *(Shouting.)* Don't forget to write. Or telephone. Every week. Twice a week. Oh God. You promised, don't you forget it.

(Lights, music, people moving.)

MAN: *(To WOMAN.)* So tell me, what is it you really want?

(WOMAN whispers something inaudible in his ear.)

Yeah, well.

(Lights, music, people moving.)

WOMAN IN GYPSY DRESS: God, I could die, I'm so happy ... I can't stand it. This is my home. My turf, my place. I never thought I'd get back here. I could—I could kiss the ground ... I wonder if—no, I couldn't— or maybe ... why not?

> *(She stoops and kisses the ground. The lights change; people wander off, leaving only a young PEOPLE-WATCHER on a bench at centre stage. She eases her backpack onto the bench and places it beside her. She is in her early twenties, dressed with a moderate smartness that suggests she has recently left the student life and is about to begin the real thing. Her random thoughts are either read by voice-over or said by her. She holds a book on her lap, but looks around the empty stage continually, furtively, appraisingly, touching her face, her body scarcely moving—the ultimate people-watcher.)*

PEOPLE-WATCHER: God! *(Pause.)* If I had one wish ... this bench! *(Pause.)* Why can't they have soft chairs in airports ... good thing I brought a book ... to pass the time ... a book can be your best companion, that's what Miss Newbury used to say back in sixth grade. Miss Blueberry we called her behind her—*(She looks around.)* Hmmm, he's attractive ... for his age ... nice necktie ... looks like he keeps in shape, probably jogs or something, tennis maybe, with that tan—but green socks! His wife maybe bought them for him, or his mother, or one of his kids ... if he has kids, which he probably does, he's as old as Dad ... well, almost ... but green! And that looks like the *Financial Post* under his arm, you'd think if he reads the *Financial Post*, he'd know about green socks, yeech ... at least they're dark green. *(Pause.)* Two hours is a long time. One hundred and twenty minutes. *(Pause.)* My new watch looks great, makes my wrist look sort of thin, kind of casual, but not too casual. I've really changed this year, my life's really ... well ... I'm older this year, more in control, sort of—a year ago I'd be sitting here worrying about how I looked and all that, and now I look like ... like ... someone who's ... sort of got it together. *(Pause.)* Here I am, reading

Crime and Punishment, Dostoyevsky, a year ago I'd be flipping through some magazine, just flipping through ... *Flipping.*

Oh, gross, too many chains, some people are so unaware what they look like, gross!

If I had one wish I'd—oh! I love it, *I love it,* she's so ... everything matches, shoes, suit, blouse, sort of, what do you call that look? mono-chromatic ... she's so pulled together, probably spent a week planning what she'd wear on the plane, laying it all out on the bed. *(Pause.)* Wonder what her bedroom looks like, lots of mirrors, I bet, track lighting, silky bedspread ... it's neat, everyone in the world has a bedroom ... or part of a bedroom, every last person ... I wish I could go up to that man over there in the white pants and say, "Hey, what's your bedroom like?" Or that girl with the chains, "What's *your* bedroom like? I mean, have you got wallpaper or what? Have you got a four-poster maybe or ..." God, I really liked that Japanese bed of Bobby's, that mattress thing, not that I'd buy one, but now and then ... and if I decide to get a place of my own and—ugh, no spare me, give *moi* a break, bedroom slippers in the airport! ... *embroidered* bedroom slip-pers, *gold* embroidery. *(Pause.)* She must be a hundred years old.

They must notice it, people must notice how they're getting older and older—like we're all getting older, right the minute you're born, you start getting ... your skin gets older and your fingernails get older, even your eyebrows get older, and when you breathe out, you're *breathing out old breath* —if only they didn't have to dress like that, why can't someone tell them, those old-lady coats with one giant button in the middle. He's sort of interesting ... maybe a little macho ... machismo ... macho-mio. *(She rolls the word around in her mouth.)* I think he's looking at me—he is! What would happen if he wandered over here and sort of looked down and said, "Hey, not only are you an attractive woman, but you're reading *Crime and Punishment,* my favourite book"—or something along those lines ... and I'd say, "Well, I sort of, you know, I'm into the Russians at the moment ..." or maybe ...

(She looks around.)

If I had one wish, I'd wish I was really gorgeous, only not dumb. I'd be able to talk about politics and stuff, nuclear disarmament ... that time I got a B+ on my essay on Argentina and Mr. Griffiths wrote "lively and provocative." *(Pause.)* That poor kid, I know just how he feels, you can tell he hates his haircut, the way he's holding his head, all stiff like a robot, do I ever know how he feels—if I get in line behind him I could say something nonchalant like, "Hey, do you mind if I ask who cuts your hair? You look great" ... something like that ... or I could say, "Look, not to worry, it'll grow out, that's one thing about hair." Ha, that time Mom gave me the home perm and I had to wear a scarf to school for a

week while the frizz settled down ... a soft perm it was supposed to be—
I probably thought the whole world was looking at me and all the time
everyone was just worrying about how they looked, that's the way
people are. If I started all of a sudden vibrating right here in the airport,
no one would come running up and say, "Hey, why's this woman
suddenly vibrating?" They wouldn't ... they probably wouldn't even
notice, or, if they did, they'd just say, "Well, she probably vibrates all the
time, that's the way she is."

At least I don't look like *that.* She probably thought it looked nice on the
hanger or something or maybe it was a present ... that time Bobby and
Marcie gave me that sweater with the bumble-bee stitched on the front,
a pink bumble-bee with little sparkles. *(She looks around.)* I don't
believe it, they're kissing ... like they don't even notice there's anyone
else around—I wish ... Oh, my God, he's probably leaving, maybe he
got transferred ... or maybe she's the one who's leaving, that looks like
her luggage, not his, white vinyl. She's not crying, tell me she's not
crying. Tears. Tears in an airport—they really, really love each other,
you can tell. *(Pause.)* If only ... oh, how I long, how I long—*(Staring.)*
Is that plastic or leather? Could be leather ... no plastic ... or maybe ...
leather—now that's Mr. Weird! He must of got the conditioner mixed up
with the shampoo, he's so conditioned he's about to explode, talk about
thick hair—to think I used to walk around blowing bubble gum like that,
what a goof, and thinking I looked so cool in my denim jacket when I
looked like—what a cute little kid ... I remember being just that size and
my mouth came up to the counter like that ... *He's licking the edge of the
counter*—I was that size for years and years and I used to ... lick the
counter ... did I really?

Droopy! Are they ever droopy, how do they get that droopy, from not
wearing a bra probably, it makes you feel droopy just looking at them
drooping away—that man with the tennis racquet, I wish he'd come over
here and start a conversation ... don't tell me he's with that other guy ...
oh no! They're not ... they're maybe ... together ... the story of my life.
(Pause.) If I had one wish ...

   (PILOT and FLIGHT ATTENDANT enter and freeze.)

Now he's sensational, it's the uniform ... very, very nice ... and those
eyes ... pilots make more than eighty thou a year, more than stock-
brokers, that was in *Time* magazine—that must be a stewardess he's
talking to—only they don't call them that anymore, what do you call
them? *(Pause.)* Flight Attendants. They look like they've really got it
together, relationship-wise, like they're really in synch, like their hearts
are beating at the same rate or something—I can feel my heart beating.
When I think of all the hearts in this airport!—we can't see them, we
can't hear them, but they're all thumping away, kaboom, kaboom,

kaboom, hundreds of them. Oh God, I feel so lonely sitting here ... I can't stand it. Maybe a cup of coffee or something ... *(She gets up and puts on her backpack.)* ... maybe a muffin, something sweet, a chocolate bar. *(Pause.)* If I had one wish ...

(The PILOT and FLIGHT ATTENDANT appear in four contretemps scenes throughout the play, standing always in the same, very tight spotlit space at stage front. The lighting and musical background separate these contretemps from the other reality of the play, evoking the "soap-operish" or "true romance" aspect of the airport. Organ music might help underline the melodramatic content. The two characters appear suddenly, and are just as suddenly blacked out.)

PILOT: How 'bout a movie?

FLIGHT ATTENDANT: Afraid not. Not tonight.

PILOT: A drink then. A quickie?

FLIGHT ATTENDANT: I'm terribly sorry. I'd like to, but—

PILOT: But you're busy. Is that right?

FLIGHT ATTENDANT: I suppose you might ... yes. That's it. I'm afraid ... I'm busy.

PILOT: And you're busy tomorrow night, right?

FLIGHT ATTENDANT: Well, yes.

PILOT: And next weekend?

FLIGHT ATTENDANT: Look, I'm sorry, but—

PILOT: Let me tell you what I sense. I sense we're—now how can I put this?—I sense we're drifting apart.

FLIGHT ATTENDANT: We hardly know each other, how can we drift—

PILOT: But we were starting to ... know each other. Didn't you feel it? That night at the Japanese restaurant? Don't tell me you didn't feel anything.

FLIGHT ATTENDANT: It was—

PILOT: It was magic. Say it. Two people with everything in common, their lives enmeshed.

FLIGHT ATTENDANT: Well—

PILOT: And now you're all of a sudden tied up every night of the week.

FLIGHT ATTENDANT: I wish I could explain, but—

PILOT: But what? There's gotta be a reason.

FLIGHT ATTENDANT: There is.

PILOT: Well, then?

FLIGHT ATTENDANT: There's a reason, but, well, I think you might find it hard to accept.

PILOT: I see. It's something about me that you find—

FLIGHT ATTENDANT: No, it's about me. And really about you too. I can't explain.

(Pause.)

PILOT: I see. I see.

(Light snaps off on PILOT and FLIGHT ATTENDANT. Two couples enter from opposite sides. The two women, JANICE and RACHEL, are seeing their husbands, JIM and ROBERT, off on a plane which is being announced by the PA in the background.)

PA: Flight 89 now boarding at Gate 2. Flight 89 for Toronto now boarding.

JANICE: *(To JIM.)* Now promise you'll phone Alice if you get a chance.

JIM: I'll try. I said I'll try. But there're going to be meetings all day—

JANICE: She'd love to hear from you. She always loves it when—

JIM: And meetings in the evenings. Plus sales seminars. Plus two official lunches and a banquet—

JANICE: She's the only sister you've got. If she ever found out you went to Toronto and didn't call—

JIM: I'll try. I said I would, didn't I?

JANICE: I know she'd appreciate it. Five minutes. It'd mean the world.

RACHEL: *(To ROBERT.)* Good luck. It'll go fine.

ROBERT: Look, will you take the car in for a lube job while I'm away?

RACHEL: I'm sure there's nothing to be nervous about. It isn't as if they're calling you into Main Office to—

ROBERT: And tell them to do a good job this time. The last time they gave it to some jerk who didn't know the hell what he was doing—

RACHEL: Let's see. Thursday night, Flight 450. I'll be here.

ROBERT: You can tell them I was not pleased. Not at all pleased.

PA: Flight 86 now boarding, Flight 86 now boarding. Step lively for Flight 86.

JANICE: Give Alice my love.

ROBERT: And get them to check the goddamn muffler.

(JIM and ROBERT go up the "Departures" steps, one a little ahead of the other. JANICE and RACHEL go over to a booth that sells flight insurance. There is a smiling ATTENDANT behind the booth.)

ATTENDANT: *(To JANICE.)* Can I help you?

JANICE: *(To RACHEL.)* I believe you were first.

RACHEL: No, you were first. I'm in no hurry.

JANICE: Well, that's very kind. *(To ATTENDANT.)* I'd like the one-million-dollar policy.

ATTENDANT: If you'll just fill in this form.

RACHEL: I'll have the million-dollar policy too. That's the one I always get.

JANICE: I do too. It seems a little silly, I know, but Jim, that's my husband, travels an awful lot.

RACHEL: So does Robert. And it's not silly at all. It's common sense.

JANICE: I can't help worrying about him.

(The two women continue their discussion standing near the insurance booth, or perhaps sitting on a bench.)

RACHEL: I'm an awful worry-wart myself. If Robert knew I worried the way I do, he'd probably stop flying. He doesn't even know I buy insurance when he flies.

JANICE: My Jim doesn't either. He'd think I was morbid. He'd think it was a waste of money. He thinks flying across the country is safer than driving down Portage Avenue.

RACHEL: Isn't that amazing! You won't believe this, but Robert says exactly the same thing.

JANICE: Jim would think I was downright neurotic if he knew I bought insurance every time he went up.

RACHEL: I never let on to Robert. I buy the million-dollar policy every time.

JANICE: Me too. I have for years.

RACHEL: What a coincidence.

JANICE: You have to think about how you would manage. If.

RACHEL: You sure as hell do.

JANICE: Lots of women have been left standing with just the change in their purse. They don't think ahead.

RACHEL: They don't think it will happen to them.

JANICE: Well, I know better. I know the statistics. I read that article, in *Newsweek.*

RACHEL: It only makes sense. If you spend enough time in the air—

JANICE: —your number's bound to come up.

RACHEL: Exactly.

JANICE: It's a responsibility, taking out insurance, that's how I look at it.

(Pause.)

RACHEL: The way I look at it, say I get the full million. I'd put half of it in short-term investment certificates, shopping around, of course, for the best interest rate—

JANICE: Oh, you have to shop around.

RACHEL: —and one-quarter into government bonds—you can't go wrong there.

JANICE: That's what I'd do, government bonds.

RACHEL: —and the remaining quarter I'd sink into a good energy stock. I figure that way I'd be getting a decent tax break.

JANICE: I think I heard Jim saying something about the energy market being risky.

RACHEL: Robert says the same thing, but that's crazy. Energy's the future.

JANICE: You'd probably have a house to maintain too.

RACHEL: Well, I've thought about that, and you know, I think I'd ... you know, if something ... happened ... if Robert, you know ... I think I'd put the house up for sale.

JANICE: Really? You think that's wise?

RACHEL: What I picture is one of those new condos on Wellington Crescent.

JANICE: Wonderful view from some of those condos.

RACHEL: And look at it this way. When you want to go away in the winter, you just shut the door ... and go!

JANICE: We don't usually go away in the winter. Once we went to Bermuda but—

RACHEL: Winter's Robert's busiest time, so we don't get away either. But if I was on my own, I'd—this probably sounds batty—but I've always wanted to see Australia. And New Zealand.

JANICE: Not me. I'd head back to Bermuda. Those beautiful beaches! Jim thought they were all out for his money, but I—

RACHEL: Well, if you went into a condo—like me—you could get away to Bermuda any time you liked. Just shut the door.

JANICE: I think what I'd do is subdivide.

RACHEL: Subdivide?

JANICE: The house, I mean. I mean, if Jim ... if ... well, I've had this idea for years. All I need is the second floor for my personal use. I'd have to close off the stairs and ... of course I'd have to get a really good architect. But it's a big house. I figure I could get four apartments out of it easily.

RACHEL: Why not? Maximize your income. And you'd have your own little apartment.

JANICE: I think I might do it in tones of gold and green.

RACHEL: Nice. Very nice.

JANICE: I'd probably want to refurnish too. You know, go in for something lighter. Wicker maybe. We have all this heavy furniture from Jim's mother's side, and well, it would be a terrible wrench parting with it—

RACHEL: An emotional wrench.

JANICE: But if Jim's ... not here ... and I know he'd want me to be comfortable.

RACHEL: I think Robert feels the same. When your life alters radically, you have to make radical adjustments.

JANICE: One thing for sure is I'd buy a waterbed.

RACHEL: What a good idea! They say they're wonderful for your back, but Robert thinks—

JANICE: Jim says they make him seasick, gurgle, gurgle all night. We had one in our hotel in Bermuda and I loved it. It was a funny thing, but I had the most wonderful dreams in that bed. And I mean ... wonderful. The kind of dreams I haven't had since ... I don't know when.

RACHEL: In that case, I think you should definitely go ahead and get the waterbed.

JANICE: And I'd have a very good reading light put in. Jim hates it when I read in bed—

RACHEL: So does Robert, he makes a great big fuss, says the light keeps him awake. And I love to read.

JANICE: So do I. But Jim—

RACHEL: As a matter of fact, I think I'd probably go back to university.

JANICE: Really!

RACHEL: Well, once I move into the condo and invest the money from the insurance, I'd have to have something to do. I mean, I can't spend all my time travelling around Australia and New Zealand.

JANICE: So you'd get a degree?

RACHEL: I'd have to do that first. But then—

JANICE: Then?

RACHEL: Then ... this may seem weird ... but I thought I'd go into social work.

JANICE: Social work! That sounds fascinating.

RACHEL: Robert always says social workers are a bunch of do-gooders, but—

JANICE: But ... if Robert wasn't here ...

RACHEL: I think I have it in me to help people.

JANICE: I think what I'd do is open a china shop. A sort of boutique, you know. Just very, very good things.

RACHEL: You could have a bridal register.

JANICE: Oh, I'd have to have a bridal register. I know times are bad, but—

RACHEL: —but people are still getting married. And you'd have the money to invest.

JANICE: And I think I have a good business head even if Jim says—

RACHEL: The world of business is fascinating.

JANICE: Full of fascinating people.

RACHEL: And it's not entirely ... well ... not impossible ... that you—or I—might meet someone. In the business world, I mean. Anything could happen.

JANICE: A man you mean?

RACHEL: Well, something like that. If someone comes along, well, why not?

JANICE: You mean ... you might remarry if ... if your husband—

RACHEL: Well, people aren't meant to be alone.

JANICE: That's what Jim always says. His sister Alice—

RACHEL: We all need companionship. I think we owe it to ourselves.

JANICE: But remarriage?

RACHEL: Maybe not remarriage. Maybe just a ... you know ... a relationship.

JANICE: A relationship. That might be an interesting thing to ... I think ... maybe ... I might consider a relationship as well.

RACHEL: *(Walking off.)* If ...

JANICE: *(Walking off in opposite direction.)* Yes, if.

PA: Ladies and gentlemen, those bound for ordinary and exotic destinations, please board. This is the final call.

(Suitcases roll down chute, and in a minute all six people come and go, down the "Arrivals" stairs. They pick up their cases and exit, leaving only the silver case and two identical white bags going around. Lights change. ALPHA and BETA, dressed identically and looking androgynous, start to reach for the bags, then pull back, exchange looks, and then let the cases go around again. They repeat this two or three times, each finally taking one.)

ALPHA: Coincidence.

BETA: Yes. It is.

ALPHA: I've never seen ... one ... like mine before.

BETA: I haven't either. I thought mine was ... the only one ... the only one there was.

ALPHA: That's what I thought too.

BETA: It's not that I haven't looked. I mean ... I really have ... looked ... but I've never seen—

ALPHA: To tell you the truth, I'd given up looking.

BETA: So had I. I was resigned.

ALPHA: Goodness!

BETA: What is it?

ALPHA: How can we be sure ... well, that this is yours and ... this is mine?

BETA: We could always—

ALPHA: Always what?

BETA: Well, I was going to suggest ... I don't want to intrude on ... to be overly personal, but I was going to suggest—

ALPHA: Please go ahead. Don't be shy.

BETA: Well, I was going to suggest that ... we ... open them.

ALPHA: Oh, I never open mine. Never.

BETA: I don't either. At least I never have before.

ALPHA: I don't think I could. I'm awfully sorry.

BETA: Have you had yours ... for a long time?

ALPHA: Well, come to think of it, it has been a long time. In fact—

BETA: I've always had mine.

ALPHA: You get so you're attached. *(Laughs.)* It's not easy ... I mean ... it's hard to think of not having one.

BETA: I know just what you mean.

ALPHA: I don't even like ... to let anyone else ... touch mine.

BETA: That's how I feel. But the truth is, well—

ALPHA: Well?

BETA: The truth is ... no one's ever touched mine.

ALPHA: Oh. In my case—

BETA: Yes, go on. You can tell me.

ALPHA: Well, the fact is, no one ... no one's ever *wanted* to touch mine.

BETA: No one?

ALPHA: No one.

BETA: Maybe—

ALPHA: Yes?

BETA: Maybe you'd let me ... touch it.

ALPHA: Oh, I don't know.

BETA: Just a little, you know, just a little pat.

ALPHA: Well, I don't suppose ... why not?

BETA: *(Touching case.)* There.

ALPHA: Oh.

BETA: That wasn't so bad, was it?

ALPHA: No. Not at all. I ... liked it. I enjoyed it.

BETA: That's good.

ALPHA: Would you like me to ... give yours ... just a little pat?

BETA: Do you think you could?

ALPHA: *(Touching case.)* There. And there.

BETA: Thank you. Very much.

ALPHA: You're welcome.

BETA: I've got an idea.

ALPHA: What?

BETA: No, never mind. Forget what I said.

ALPHA: Please.

BETA: Well, I just thought ... now if you don't like this idea, all you have
to do is—

ALPHA: I'll like it. I promise.

BETA: Well, what if I gave you mine ... and you gave me ... yours?

ALPHA: I ... I—

BETA: I hope you don't think—

ALPHA: What I was going to say is ... I think that would be wonderful.

BETA: Really?

ALPHA: Really.

BETA: Well, here you are.

ALPHA: And here you are.

BETA: Thank you.

ALPHA: Thank *you.*

BETA: Are you going this way?

ALPHA: Yes, as a matter of fact—

BETA: *(Offering an arm.)* Well, why don't we—

ALPHA: We might as well.

> *(They exit. Three REPORTERS carrying cameras enter at a run and take up positions at bottom of the "Arrivals" stairs. A number of pieces of matched red luggage comes down the chute. They are followed an instant later by a greasy backpack.)*

PA: Ladies and gentlemen, will you kindly clear the area for the arrival of an important personage.

REPORTER ONE: Where the hell is she?

REPORTER TWO: You sure her flight's in?

REPORTER THREE: That's gotta be her luggage.

REPORTER ONE: Gee, that's a lotta luggage for one day in this town.

REPORTER THREE: I didn't want this assignment. I wanted to cover the Agricultural Support Talks.

REPORTER ONE: You did?

REPORTER THREE: Some real interesting stuff coming up today on wheat quotas. And oats. Maybe even barley!

REPORTERS: *(In unison.)* Here she comes. One, two, three ready.

> *(Flashbulbs go off. At the top of the "Arrivals" stairs is large voluptuous movie star, MISS HORTON-HOLLIS, vulgarly dressed. She does several poses as cameras go off.)*

MISS HORTON-HOLLIS: That'll have to do, fellas.

REPORTER ONE: Would you mind answering a few questions, Miss Horton-Hollis?

MISS HORTON-HOLLIS: I've got four minutes and I'm willing to talk about anything except my relationship with Warren Beatty—

REPORTER TWO: That's completely kaput, right?

REPORTER ONE: Is it true you're in therapy, Miss Horton-Hollis?

MISS HORTON-HOLLIS: Psychic reconstruction, unmasking the self so you can find the true core of being that—

REPORTER THREE: *(Scribbling.)* Core of being? Could you comment on that please?

MISS HORTON-HOLLIS: I'm talking about the amalgam of the absence and the presence. The intersection of innerness and outerness.

REPORTER TWO: How do you spell "amalgam"?

MISS HORTON-HOLLIS: The coming together of otherness and ethos, nature and antinature, the chicken and the egg—

REPORTER ONE: Neat.

MISS HORTON-HOLLIS: All life, you see, is a question of arrivals and departures. Of going through gateways.

REPORTER THREE: Gee, that's right. When you stop to think.

MISS HORTON-HOLLIS: You travel out as far as you can go—

REPORTER ONE: Far out!

MISS HORTON-HOLLIS: Then you turn your face one-hundred-eighty degrees and retrace your steps.

REPORTER THREE: *(Excitedly.)* Like—like—like life's kind of like, sort of, you know, a cycle ... and the custom officer sort of symbolizes, well, you know, he sort of represents—

REPORTER ONE: About this thing with Warren Beatty, you say it's definitely over. We heard there was a chance of—

REPORTER THREE: *(To the others.)* This person is on a quest to the centre of being and you slobs want to talk abut some tinsel-town romance.

REPORTER ONE: All I want to know is, is it on or off?

MISS HORTON-HOLLIS: Off. But talk to me tomorrow.

(She descends and goes through the doors; an aide appears and carries her luggage. The REPORTERS keep snapping.)

REPORTER THREE: And to think I almost went to the Agricultural Support Talks—that's the problem with stereotypes, fellas, we get bounced on our heads every time.

(A young POET bounds into view and down the stairs, picks up the backpack, then turns and faces the REPORTERS.)

POET: If you'd like a statement, gentlemen—

REPORTER THREE: *(After a pause.)* You got a statement?

POET: I'll be brief. The verse is dead. The line is dead. And be sure to get this—get your pencils ready, gentlemen—the word is dead.

REPORTER ONE: And you are?

POET: It's in the press release. Poet on the road. Man with a message.

REPORTER THREE: The message again is—?

REPORTER ONE: I took a course in poetry once. The prof said all great poetry was about—

POET: The poem is about the poem is about the poem is about—

REPORTER THREE: Wait a minute, I can't write that fast.

POET: And now, if you'd like one more picture—

REPORTER THREE: Thank you.

(He takes a picture; the blinding flashbulb blacks out the stage for an

*instant. The POET and REPORTERS ONE and TWO go out through
the automatic doors, leaving REPORTER THREE on stage.)*

REPORTER THREE: *(Addressing the audience.)* There's something I'd
like to share with you out there. It's about the rich and famous. I meet
quite a few of them in my line of work. You know, there's a saying that
if you stand here, right here, at the information counter, long enough, the
whole world passes by. No kidding, it's true. I've seen it happen. But
that's not what I want to say to you. What I want to say is that the rich
and famous, well, they're just like you and me. Inside, I mean, like, deep
down, like they've got feelings. They've got bad taste in art, some of
them. They applaud in the wrong places at the symphony. They get
struck by lightning. They get hives. Hernias. Corns on their feet, know
what I'm saying?

*(Behind REPORTER THREE a tall, splendidly dressed ARAB ap-
pears.)*

If it isn't the fabulously wealthy, the near-legendary, the practically
mythical … *(Confiding to the audience.)* travelling incognito, of course,
but get a load of that ruby ring. Excuse me, folks.

*(He hurries after the ARAB, who exits through the automatic doors.
As they leave, a TELEPHONER enters and goes to the pay phone.)*

TELEPHONER: *(Dials.)* Mom? Yes, it's me. No, it's not Andy, it's Bob.
Must be a bad connection. I said, it's me. It's Bob. Bobby. No, I'm not
kidding, it's me. I'm right here in town. Out at the airport. I'm on my
way to Calgary. No, a business trip! Well, I was going to write and let
you know, but I'm only here for a twenty-five-minute stopover and I
didn't want you coming all the way out from the house just for—what?
No. No, Mom. I haven't seen Andy lately. Well, Toronto's a big city,
and I just haven't seen him for a couple of months or so. No, he looked
fine, I thought, same old Andy. I'll tell him, Mom, but you know he was
never one for letters. I'll just tell him to give you a phone call, okay?
Anyway, Mom, I just wanted to let you know Irene and the kids are fine.
Sandy's just had his birthday. We took all the kids in the neighbourhood
over to McDonald's and they had a ball. You should have seen Sandy all
surrounded by—what? No, not that I know of, Mom. I don't think so,
Mom. No. Mom? Well, look, Mom, I can't just call him up and say, do
you have a girlfriend? I know he's my brother, but Jesus, Mom. Why
don't you write him and ask him then? *(Pause.)* And what did he say?
Oh, I think you worry too much, Mom. Irene says … Irene! My wife. She
says Andy isn't ready to settle down. Well, thirty-two's not exactly over
the hill and when the time comes—you've *got* grandchildren, Mom.
You've got Sandy and Missy and Muffy and they all send you hugs and
kisses, Mom. The last thing Muffy said at the airport—it was the cutest
darned thing—she said, "Tell Grammy I lof her a lot." He's … yes … as

far as I know, Mom. Yes, the same address. No, he hasn't moved. What makes you think he's moved? Yes, I think so, the two of them. Well, I don't know, Mom. How can I tell what kind of influence he has on Andy, you can't lump all interior decorators together—I'll try. Okay. I promise, but he's a big boy, I can't tell him how to run his life, but I'll have a talk ... I can't this week, Mom. Because I'm on my way to Calgary. We're opening a new branch and ... Mom, I know you worry. Look, you're getting all worked up for—he's happy, he's got his life. Well, he's probably happy. Well, he could be. No one's happy all the time. Jesus! I gotta go. I really ... bye Mom.

(He exits. The PA makes an announcement, the specifics of which are inaudible.)

PA: Flight [inaudible] has been delayed due to [inaudible]. Attention all passengers on flight [inaudible]. Because of [inaudible] we will be delayed for two hours, and passengers are asked to [inaudible].

(A FRENCHMAN dressed in a European style enters. He speaks with a French accent.)

FRENCHMAN: *Zut!* Two hours. This is a *catastroph*. I am expected. I am anticipated.

(A BRITISH MATRON enters, speaking with a British accent.)

BRITISH MATRON: But this is intolerable. Not to be tolerated. Surely they don't expect one to tolerate—

(A woman, DOROTHY, enters. She is young but already matronly.)

DOROTHY: Oh, dear, what next? First the handle of my suitcase breaks? Just snaps in two? And now?

(A young JOCK enters, a beer-drinker sort.)

JOCK: Hey, this's gotta be—I mean, we put a guy on the moon, but we can't put a—

(An elderly POLITICIAN enters.)

POLITICIAN: This is an outrage. The committee will hear about this. Heads will roll. I intend to file a formal report.

DOROTHY: A refund maybe?

FRENCHMAN: And *apologé* perhaps, no?

BRITISH MATRON: Shocking inconvenience.

JOCK: Yeah, sort of like, shocking.

POLITICIAN: I'm going to insist on a meal voucher.

FRENCHMAN: Or a drink *peut être*.

BRITISH MATRON: Sherry! A dry sherry.

DOROTHY: Gee, a cuppa coffee would sure go down.

(A FLIGHT ATTENDANT enters with a tray of styrofoam cups.)

FLIGHT ATTENDANT: My apologies, ladies and gentlemen, for the delay. The airline has authorized, I am happy to say, a cup of coffee for each and every inconvenienced passenger.

POLITICIAN: Well, I should hope so.

JOCK: Hey, great!

FRENCHMAN: *Magnifique.*

BRITISH MATRON: Splendid.

JOCK: Hey, you know something, there's nothing—nothing!—like the smell of coffee.

DOROTHY: That's for sure.

FRENCHMAN: *Ah, ça sent bon!*

POLITICIAN: Fresh brewed aroma.

FLIGHT ATTENDANT: The best smell on this earth.

(All raise their cups and drink; a short silence follows.)

FRENCHMAN: Well ... there are some peoples, and I believe I am one, who hold the opinion that the best smell in the world is—

BRITISH MATRON: Yes?

FRENCHMAN: It is only my opinion, of course, but perhaps you have on occasion walked through a virgin forest, no? Early in the morning. After a little fall of rain. *(He sniffs deeply.)* It is, how you say, the perfume of nature, the aroma of the earth, an experience that is unrivalled in this world.

JOCK: Yeah, man.

BRITISH MATRON: Speaking personally, I can't help remembering—now I expect this is going to sound absurd—but I do distinctly remember—from my childhood—the smell of liver and bacon frying.

POLITICIAN: I beg your pardon.

BRITISH MATRON: This was during the war years, you understand, a time of courage and deprivation. We had strict rationing, so many ounces of meat per week. A difficult time, you have no idea, but we came to appreciate small things. Humble things. And one day, a cold, damp day, January, I believe, I returned from my school. I was twelve, thirteen, a child really—

FRENCHMAN: But it is children who appreciate the—

BRITISH MATRON: I let myself in the door and at once was struck by a veritable gale of sensation. Liver and bacon. My mother stood in the kitchen with a meat fork in hand. She was like, like a priestess. And from the smoking fry pan beside her came a smell which has always seemed to me to be supreme in the world of smells. A kingly smell. I don't expect any of you to understand but—

JOCK: *(Sincerely.)* I guess it's like you kinda hadda be there, eh?

(The POLITICIAN clears his throat noisily.)

POLITICIAN: My father was a man of simple but severe tastes. A traditionalist in the finest sense. We were far from being affluent and made do with countless small economies. But a single luxury was permitted: my father's white shirts were sent out to be laundered. Seven shirts every week. No, on second thought, it was six, he made his Friday shirt do for Saturday as well. Wonderful man. Well, as a boy, I was given the task of fetching his shirts. The laundry—they no longer exist, not the same— was tiny, crowded, steamy—and the smell! How can I describe it?

BRITISH MATRON: The smell of cleanliness.

FLIGHT ATTENDANT: Scorched cotton.

DOROTHY: Starch? Bleach?

FRENCHMAN: I know also this heavenly smell.

JOCK: Hey, me too, in a way.

POLITICIAN: That smell held both the security of the present and the possibility of the future. Tradition and dignity. Comfort and order. The finest smell in the world.

JOCK: I kinda know what you mean, but—

POLITICIAN: But what, my boy?

JOCK: I mean, yeah, clean smells are great, but sometimes, well, it's hard to describe, but—

BRITISH MATRON: Try.

JOCK: Well, it's like, I've played a little hockey, well, a lot of hockey, like I started when I was, jeez, I must've been four years old, something like that. My dad took me down to the rink and signed me up and there I was, thinking I was going to be a star, playing for the Blackhawks or something—

FRENCHMAN: It is a most interesting game, this hockey.

JOCK: Yeah, well, a lotta kids, when they grow out of their skates, they take 'em to this second-hand place, but my dad, he saved my old skates, he's kind of—

DOROTHY: Sentimental?

JOCK: Yeah, like that, sentimental. Anyway, he's got this cardboard box down the basement full of my old stinky skates, little bitty ones this long, right up to the size twelves I wore when we won the provincials—well, all I can say is, the smell of old ice skates is just about, well, it's the smell of all smells.

FLIGHT ATTENDANT: You know, what I love is the smell of a party, going to a party, when you first get there. You stand in the hall, and it's partly cold and partly warm and you can smell all the boots lined up there, and there's a kind of chip-and-dip breeze blowing in from the living room, and cologne and after-shave—

DOROTHY: Once … once—

(DOROTHY pauses. The others prompt and encourage her to continue.)

Well, my husband? He travels a fair amount? He's a, you know, a consultant? He goes all over the place, all over the world? And, well, usually he comes home with this suitcase just chuck full, just bulging with dirty socks and underwear and stuff? I open it up and, whew! Well—

(She pauses and the others prod her once more.)

Well, last year he went to Mali? That's in Africa? Where they speak the French language.

FRENCHMAN: That is true.

DOROTHY: Well, he got home and I opened his suitcase, expecting I'd see the same old bunch of dirty underwear? Only, what I didn't know was … he'd had it all washed there in the hotel? They wash stuff by hand, he said, and hang it on the bushes in the back of the hotel to dry. I couldn't believe it, what my nose was smelling. It was …

BRITISH MATRON: *(Wisely.)* The smell of purity.

FRENCHMAN: Fresh linen, nothing like it.

DOROTHY: No, no, it wasn't that. It *was* that, and more? I buried my nose in all those clean, white, folded-up clothes, and what I was smelling, I realized all of a sudden, was Africa. *(Pause. She looks from face to face.)* I could smell … Africa!

JOCK: Excellent, hey, that's—

BRITISH MATRON: *(Dreamily.)* The smell of cold metal, water pipes, and swings in the park. Doorknobs.

POLITICIAN: A nice new newspaper when you open it, nothing can beat—

FRENCHMAN: Or an old newspaper—

JOCK: Peanut butter when you first open it, that second when you zip the top off—

FRENCHMAN: Anything you have to work hard to open. It smells best when you have to work at it, getting the cork out of the—

JOCK: Someone with a new haircut smells great; they smell sort of crisp-like. Like you know that haircut hasn't been slept in yet, nothing bad's happened to it.

DOROTHY: Wallpaper paste?

FLIGHT ATTENDANT: Christmas tree ornaments when you bring them down from the attic—

POLITICIAN: But the best smell—are you listening?—the best smell is a combination of smells. Like ... like brandy and wet wool, like when you come in from being heroic—

BRITISH MATRON: *(Dreamily again.)* Boiled cabbage and cooking gas.

JOCK: Erasers, wow! With lockers and dirty jeans.

FRENCHMAN: And what I find so, so marvellous, is that each of us, we each have a smell that is all our own.

> *(A sudden silence falls; each of the six stiffens and contracts and stares upward.)*

PA: Flight [inaudible] for [inaudible] is now ready to board. Will passengers for [inaudible] please go to Gate [inaudible].

FLIGHT ATTENDANT: If you will follow me, please—

> *(All rise from the bench and follow her; conversation begins again, random and overlapping.)*

POLITICIAN: Popcorn. An old-fashioned bowl of—

BRITISH MATRON: When you polish a fine piece of furniture—

JOCK: Coffee, boy, a fresh cuppa coffee sure—

> *(Exit all. Enter PILOT and FLIGHT ATTENDANT in their second "true-romance" contretemps, spotlighted, same position as in the first contretemps.)*

PILOT: Well, hello!

FLIGHT ATTENDANT: Hello.

PILOT: I know.

FLIGHT ATTENDANT: You know what?

PILOT: About it. I know all about it. Everything there is to know, I know.

FLIGHT ATTENDANT: It?

PILOT: Why you're so busy every night.

FLIGHT ATTENDANT: Oh.

PILOT: I don't see how you expected me not to find out about something like this ... keep *this* a secret from me.

FLIGHT ATTENDANT: I didn't want to hurt you. I knew you wouldn't be able to understand.

PILOT: How could I not understand?

FLIGHT ATTENDANT: That night in the Japanese restaurant. Do you remember?

PILOT: As if I could ever forget that night.

FLIGHT ATTENDANT: Do you remember, we were talking, everything was going so—and then you told me what you thought about women who—

PILOT: Go on.

FLIGHT ATTENDANT: About women ... training for their ... pilot's papers. About women having no place in the air.

PILOT: In the cockpit is what I said. The cockpit.

FLIGHT ATTENDANT: Exactly.

PILOT: You're the best flight attendant working for this airline and now suddenly you want—

FLIGHT ATTENDANT: This is something I've always wanted.

PILOT: But why?

FLIGHT ATTENDANT: This is my dream. I was hoping ... hoping you might share it with—

PILOT: Why did it have to come to—just when—why must you—

(Lights snap off. They exit as a middle-aged MAN and his DAUGHTER, a young woman, enter.)

MAN: You've got a few minutes, honey.

DAUGHTER: I know.

MAN: Unless you'd rather go through now.

DAUGHTER: Not unless—

MAN: Unless what?

DAUGHTER: I mean, you know, there's no need for you to stick around. These farewells are so ... phoney. No one knows what to say. Well, maybe they do, but they don't say it.

MAN: I think you're right. Why is that, I wonder. We talk and talk, and then, at the last minute, we act as though we're scared of each other.

DAUGHTER: We think we have to say something big. Something important, that's the problem. And it's hard to think of important things, we just think of dumb things.

MAN: Like, did you pack your winter coat? Do you have your money in a safe place? Do you, by the way? Your money?

DAUGHTER: For heaven's sake, Dad—

MAN: And what about your down jacket? Vancouver's not all that balmy.

DAUGHTER: You see what I mean?

MAN: I suppose what I should do is give you some advice.

DAUGHTER: Advice?

MAN: Fatherly advice. But I guess the last thing you want is advice.

DAUGHTER: That's not true. I think I'd like some advice. Something primal and wise from the great treasure house of age.

MAN: I'm not sure I can live up to that.

DAUGHTER: Just shoot.

MAN: You mean it?

DAUGHTER: Why not?

MAN: My golden opportunity. Do you know, in your twenty-two years you've never asked me for advice?

DAUGHTER: Did you ever ask *your* father for advice?

(Pause.)

MAN: Only once.

DAUGHTER: Well, here's your chance. Give me some advice. I won't promise to take it. Just to listen.

MAN: I suppose that's something.

DAUGHTER: Well, then?

MAN: The problem is—

DAUGHTER: *(Mocking.)* Reluctance overtakes him. The subject is too delicate to broach.

MAN: No, it's not that. I guess I'd have to think about it a little more.

DAUGHTER: What you're saying is, you don't have any advice for me.

MAN: You sound disappointed.

DAUGHTER: You know something, I am.

MAN: I guess I do have a question at least.

DAUGHTER: Well, I suppose that's better than nothing.

MAN: Okay, here it comes. Are you sure he's the one?

DAUGHTER: Listen, I thought you were going to ask me something new. Not just is he the one? You and Mom have been asking me that for three weeks steady.

MAN: I know. But now I'm really asking. It's just you and me, you and your old man, and we've got six minutes before you get on that plane, and you can still cash in your tickets, and you can put through a phone call or send a FAX if that's easier, or—

DAUGHTER: Look, give me a break—

MAN: I mean, you say you're sure, but—

DAUGHTER: Let me ask you a question. What exactly do you mean by that little word, "sure?"

MAN: I mean, do you feel it? Do you feel that absolute certainty that there's a future—

DAUGHTER: Well, shit, when it comes right down to it, there's not an awful lot anyone can be a hundred percent sure of. I could crash on that plane for instance. You could have an accident just driving home. We can't even be sure of the next five minutes. Some crazy could come along and toss a bomb at us—

MAN: Listen, I'm asking you, do you, from time to time, have doubts?

DAUGHTER: Well, sure, I've got the odd little doubt now and then, everyone has doubts—

MAN: It's a big step. I've seen lives ruined because people get locked into things they're not sure of.

DAUGHTER: You don't like him. Is that it? I mean, basically, is that it?

MAN: My liking him or not liking him is immaterial.

DAUGHTER: What exactly is it about him? Is it because he didn't send me a Christmas present? Big deal. He doesn't believe in Christmas presents. He thinks that's a lot of pagan bullshit.

MAN: Look, there are three more minutes, so I'm going to try this on you once more. Are you sure?

DAUGHTER: You're trying to wear me down.

MAN: I love you, that's all.

DAUGHTER: I love you too. I just wish—

MAN: What?

DAUGHTER: I wish you'd get it through your head that things are different now. Say it doesn't work out. It's not like it was in your day. You don't have to stick it out forever. You don't have to spend the rest of your life paying for it.

MAN: Is that what you really think?

DAUGHTER: I'm just saying—if. That's a big if. I'm not saying it's not going to work out.

MAN: You do feel pretty sure then?

DAUGHTER: How sure was Mom when you got married?

MAN: She was sure.

DAUGHTER: I'll bet she was. Well, those days were simpler in a way.

MAN: I won't ask you again.

DAUGHTER: Is it because he works out in a health club?

MAN: I was sure too.

DAUGHTER: Is it because he sells computers? We can't all—

MAN: We were both sure, your mother and I.

DAUGHTER: We've opted for an entrepreneurial society and someone has to—

MAN: We were engaged for almost three years. That's what people did then. So they'd be sure.

DAUGHTER: He talks to me about computers, takes me into his world. That's what's important in a relationship—

MAN: When we got married it was forever. That's why we had to be so sure. Or else—ah, but you aren't listening to me, are you?

DAUGHTER: I'm listening, I'm listening. But I guess, I guess I've got a question for you. Why in God's name have you and Mom stuck it out all these years?

MAN: I said—

DAUGHTER: And whatever you tell me, please, please don't say it was for my sake.

MAN: We naturally felt—

DAUGHTER: Because I couldn't bear that, that would break my heart if I thought—

MAN: Your mother and I—

PA: Flight 411 boarding for Vancouver at Gate—

MAN: I suppose it's just that your mother and I believed—

DAUGHTER: Listen, Daddy, you don't have to stick it out any longer. Look at me, I'm twenty-two years old. I've grown up, I'm off on my own. You don't have to hang in there for the rest of your—

MAN: There've been lots of good times—

DAUGHTER: How many? One good time? Two good times?

MAN: A few, a few.

DAUGHTER: A few isn't enough. No one should settle for a few good times. Believe me, I'm not about to settle for—

MAN: You're going to miss your plane.

DAUGHTER: I know. I have to go.

MAN: And I never gave you any advice.

DAUGHTER: *(Shrugging.)* Well, did your father give you any advice when you got married?

   (Pause.)

MAN: He did give me some advice, yes. It was the only time, I think, he ever did.

DAUGHTER: And did you take it?

(Pause.)

MAN: Yes. I did.

DAUGHTER: I can just guess what kind of advice he gave you.

MAN: Sweetie, you've got one minute.

DAUGHTER: I think he took you aside and said, "Son, you've got to do the honourable thing."

MAN: Look, you've—

DAUGHTER: He said, "You got this lovely sweet young girl in trouble and you've got to do the honourable thing and make her your wife." *(Pause.)* I've known for years. Ever since I could add and subtract. So you did the honourable thing, didn't you? Oh, Daddy.

MAN: Those were different days.

DAUGHTER: And look what you got. You were noble and honourable and you got nothing.

MAN: I got you, sweetie.

DAUGHTER: That's pretty corny. That's bullshit.

MAN: Maybe it is. But maybe it's true. You know, if things don't work out … you can always come back. We'll be here.

DAUGHTER: But you don't have to be here. You haven't been listening to a word I've said, have you? I just said—

MAN: And I just said, we'll be here. Just keep that in mind. In case.

DAUGHTER: I've got to go.

MAN: *(Calling after her.)* Be happy. Be kind to each other.

DAUGHTER: Hey, that sounds like advice. Thanks.

MAN: *(Calling.)* You're welcome. It's free.

> *(They exit. A woman of about sixty, MRS KITCHELL of Rosy Rapids, comes to centre stage. She settles herself on a bench, loosens her coat, checks her watch, pulls out knitting from her bag which is on the floor.)*

MRS KITCHELL: *(Addressing the audience directly.)* I'm early. *(She fishes in her bag for a pattern.)* Quite early. As a matter of fact, I'm two hours early. My father was the same, always early, only of course he travelled by train. He worked for Timothy Eaton's, a buyer in ladies' shoes, did quite a bit of gadding about, here and there, always off some place. He liked to get down to the station in plenty of time. "You never know," that's how he put it. Meaning, you never know what could happen.

I was up at six-thirty this morning. Had my breakfast, *(She fishes in her bag.)* Bran Flakes, then a cup of tea. *(More fishing.)* Mr. Skelton picked

me up at eight sharp. Lovely new car he has, even smells new. I said,
"This is awfully nice," and he said, "What are neighbours for?" He's got
a way with words. I said, "Not many neighbours would get up at this
ungodly hour." Well, he took me all the way into Red Bluff, right to the
bus station, and said, "Well now, you sure you're going to be okay,
crossing the drink on your own?" and I said, "I sure am."

I was in plenty of time, even had time for a cup of coffee. The girl at the
counter said, "Well, well, I hear you're going all the way over to
England, Mrs Kitchell," and I said, "That's right, you heard right." *(She
rummages in her bag, takes out a tape-measure, measures her knitting,
and replaces the measure.)* I said to her—I think she was one of the
Swanson girls, the youngest—I said, "I guess you know I'm off to visit
my brand new grandson, six months old." "Is that right?" she said, and
(Pause.) gave me a look.

Well, the bus finally came along and we got into the city just about noon
and I said to myself, guess I'll pop over to Penney's. I always like to look
around Penney's, even if I don't buy, only this time I did buy—some
more wool—and then I caught my bus out to the airport and here I am.
(She holds up a sweater.) Almost done. These teensie weensie sleeves
are the devil. It's for little Moe. Moe! What a name. When I got out here
to the airport, I had to go over to the counter there and show my ticket—
it's my daughter's husband who got the idea in the first place—oh, some
time ago—of sending me a plane ticket and talking me into coming over
for a visit. We've never met, my son-in-law and myself, but we had a
nice chat on the long distance. He's got money, that's one thing, plenty
of money, well, that goes without saying. He had to say everything twice
because of his accent. "Allo Meesus Keetchell." Also he's got a lot of
family feeling, that's something. Susan says they all do. And he wanted
his little Moe to meet his grandma.

(Confidentially.) His full name is Mohammed. Now here's a very interesting fact. What is the most common first name in the world? A good
question for a quiz program. You'd probably think John or Bill or Jim,
but no, it's Mohammed. That's on account of all the Mohammedans
have to name their first sons that particular name. It's a rule like the
Catholics used to have, calling their first girls Mary, Mary Gladys or
Mary Grace, or what have you. When Susan sent the birth announcement she said, "Now Mother, be sure to put it in the local paper." Well,
I did just what she said, but I didn't put the name in. I just said, "A little
son born to Dr. and Mrs. B. Khazzi. Mrs. Khazzi is the former Susan
Kitchell of Rosy Rapids," and so on. Well, the phone half rung off the
wall, everyone wanted to know what they were going to call it, but I just
kept mum. I wasn't about to tell the whole world my daughter had a baby
named Mohammed, but after a time I kind of dropped the hint that Susan
had nicknamed the baby Moe. Mr. Skelton, he's the only one who knows

about the name Mohammed and he says it's a real nice name. Well, I wonder if ... of course he'll have dark hair, I expect that, even with Susan being so fair.

My husband Sam was dark-haired, that would be the Russian side of his family. My own family didn't know what to think when I married someone with Russian blood and a farmer to boot. But Susan took after me. I had a feeling when she went over to England for her trip that something would happen, that she'd meet someone foreign. A premonition, that's the word for it. But I didn't think this, that she'd marry ... Susan says he's real modern though, doesn't wear the cloth thing on his head. If she'd stayed home she might have married Larry Kingman who has the Macleod store, or rather his dad does. *(Pats bag.)* Larry sent her a nice wedding present, all wrapped up so nice. Looks like a nice coffeepot to me, electric maybe. Poor Larry. Looks a little, well, down in the mouth these days. Says it's a late wedding gift. *(Pats parcel.)* Says it's a sort of remembrance—so she won't ever forget him. He's a nice boy, clean living. Well, you can't run your children's lives for them, if they want to marry someone they're going to ... at least we believe in the same god, more or less, that is.

(Three young BASKETBALL PLAYERS in sports sweats enter while MRS KITCHELL is talking. One of them sets a zippered bag beside her, opens it and takes out a basketball. The three of them begin pitching it about. They dribble and move about the stage, sending the ball flying over her head. She ducks once or twice, then picks up her bag and moves to another bench. The three of them sit on a bench and pick up copies of the sports page as MRS KITCHELL continues.)

As I was saying, it took getting used to. My Susan—she was in 4-H, you know—well, I couldn't imagine, the same bed and all ... but I suppose if you turn out the light ... Sam used to turn out the light, he was very thoughtful that way. But sometimes in the summertime ... you know how long it takes for the sun to go down in the summertime ... some of the time a little light crept in through the curtains. Well, what he liked to do, well, was unbutton my nightie and then he'd, well ... suck on my bosom. It seemed like a real strange thing for a grown-up man to do, but years later I read in *McCalls* magazine or maybe in the *Digest* that it's something men ... something they like to do. Well, sometimes when it was summer and the light was getting in through the curtains, I would look down and see that black hair of Sam's, rough black hair, the Russian side, and he'd be sucking and sucking. I could see every strand of his hair so clear. I could count them almost. It was a long time ago. I've gone all saggy here, *(She touches her breasts.)* but once, well once, a long time ago I used to think, Sam and I, we're the only two people in the world who know about ... these. *(She touches her breasts again.)* And now I'm the only one.

(A woman OFFICIAL briskly approaches MRS KITCHELL. She is dressed in an official airline uniform.)

OFFICIAL: Are you Mrs Kitchell of Rosy Rapids? The lady who's going on Flight 223 to Heathrow this afternoon?

MRS KITCHELL: Why, yes, that's me.

OFFICIAL: I'm awfully sorry, Mrs Kitchell, but I have some rather disappointing news for you.

MRS KITCHELL: Why, what on earth—?

OFFICIAL: Nothing serious, nothing to worry about. Just an overbooking. It happens all the time.

MRS KITCHELL: Overbooking? Now is that when there are more people than—?

OFFICIAL: —more people than there are seats. That's it, and we're really awfully sorry—

MRS KITCHELL: You mean I won't be able to go?

OFFICIAL: All it means is that you're able to go tomorrow instead of today.

MRS KITCHELL: Tomorrow? But I was up at six-thirty and Mr. Skelton very kindly drove me all the way into Red Bluff to catch my—

OFFICIAL: We'll be happy to put you up at a nice hotel tonight.

MRS KITCHELL: But my daughter's expecting me. And little Moe.

(Another WOMAN joins them. She is slim and white-haired, and wearing boots, blue jeans, and a jean jacket.)

WOMAN: Wait a minute. Wait a minute. What's going on here? Why exactly has this particular person been bumped, if you don't mind my asking?

OFFICIAL: It's just routine. The plane to Heathrow's overbooked.

WOMAN: And why is it suddenly overbooked? It wasn't overbooked yesterday when I made my reservation.

OFFICIAL: Things happen.

WOMAN: What kind of things? It doesn't by any chance have anything to do with *(She gestures at the BASKETBALL PLAYERS.)* those animals?

OFFICIAL: This happens to be the National All Star team. They'll be playing in London, England tomorrow night, representing all of us, you and me and Mrs Kitchell here.

WOMAN: Balls. Everyone knows there are five players on a basketball team.

OFFICIAL: Oh, they never travel together. Think what would happen ...

WOMAN: *(To MRS KITCHELL.)* How long have you had your booking?

MRS KITCHELL: Well, now, let me think. My daughter's husband—he's quite well to do, a doctor—he sent me a plane ticket last ... I think it was last July. Just after little Moe was born.

WOMAN: Hear that? This woman has had her ticket since July. And these greasers come along and flex their muscles and wave their little flag and all of a sudden they're on and this passenger is off.

OFFICIAL: We'll be happy to notify Mrs Kitchell's relations in England and—

WOMAN: Listen to me, Mrs Kitchell. Don't let them do this to you. You know why they chose you to bump? They said to themselves, "Let's check the passenger list and find us a little old lady." It's called an LOL, little old lady. LOLs are pushovers. They cave in without a fight. Because LOLs have spent their lives giving in. Always accommodating, always making sure they don't make a fuss. Giving in to fathers, giving in to husbands, giving in to children. Now is that true or is it not true?

MRS KITCHELL: Well, I don't know—

WOMAN: When an LOL is faced with a direct question she says, "Well, I don't know."

OFFICIAL: I think you should know that these young athletes are going to represent our nation.

WOMAN: And who does Mrs Kitchell represent? Let me tell you, ladies and gentlemen.

(The scene now takes on the tone of a revival meeting; the three BASKETBALL PLAYERS begin to sway slowly in unison.)

Mrs Kitchell here represents the LOLs of the world. Now let me tell you loud and clear that we are not talking about some tiny piddling fraction of the universe, no ma'am. We are talking about one-sixth of the human race. Do you know how many LOLs are walking around? Look on the buses of the cities of the world. Look into the hospital wards, look into the shabby rooms of boarding houses—

BASKETBALL PLAYERS: *(In unison.)* Gee, we don't see all that many little old ladies around.

WOMAN: That's because they're little, remember?

BASKETBALL PLAYERS: *(In unison.)* Hey, that's right.

WOMAN: And when exactly did the little old ladies get little? They weren't little *young* ladies. In the beginning they were full-sized human creatures. But what happened? Well, I'll tell you what happened. They were told to keep their voices down. They were told to keep their feet together, to keep their hands on their laps, to hold their elbows in, to keep their eyes lowered, to keep their chins tucked in, to keep their heads modestly bowed, that's how they got little. And that's not all.

MRS KITCHELL: What else? What else?

WOMAN: Some of them got so little they got to be invisible. The Eskimos put their little old ladies on ice floes and set them adrift. We put ours in chimney corners and hand them a pair of knitting needles and say, "Be quiet, you." They're voiceless. They've got no guts, but I ask you, is it their fault they've got no guts?

MRS KITCHELL and OFFICIAL: No, no, no.

WOMAN: Their guts were taken away over the years, bit by bit, inch by inch. They were too fragile for sports, they were too dizzy for math, they were too unclean for church, they—

MRS KITCHELL: There was this one woman preacher last summer in Rosy Rapids—

OFFICIAL: Tokenism.

WOMAN: Their boyfriends say, "Give over." Their husbands say, "Lie back." Their sons say, "When's dinner?" They go to restaurants and they get a table by the washroom.

MRS KITCHELL, OFFICIAL and BASKETBALL PLAYERS: Yes, yes, that's right. *(Etc.)*

WOMAN: No one brings them a wine menu. All they get is a stinking pot of tea.

MRS KITCHELL: Sometimes a nice pot of tea can—

WOMAN: They join a political party and they get put on the coffee brigade. They go on trips sometimes, but, have you noticed?—they never go on journeys.

MRS KITCHELL, OFFICIAL and BASKETBALL PLAYERS: Yes, right on, bravo, amen. *(Etc.)*

WOMAN: They go out to get a job and people say, "Hey, you can't do anything or you would have done it by now. Where have you been, little old lady?" I'll tell you where they've been. Look at Mrs Kitchell from Rosy Rapids here. She can't even stand up straight. She's so used to making herself agreeable and grateful and nice nice nice that she's just faded away. And now she's being asked to give up her seat on a transatlantic jet. She was going to visit her daughter and her brand new grandson—

MRS KITCHELL: *(She throws her arms open, making a public confession.)* His name's Moe. It's short for Mohammed. And he's a real sweetie-pie, he's just the cutest bundle of—

WOMAN: Mrs Kitchell was going to visit her little grandson, taking him this sweater she's made with her own hands. The LOLs are the makers of garments, the healers of family wounds—

MRS KITCHELL: Why, that's true.

BASKETBALL PLAYERS: *(In unison.)* It's not our fault. We were just following orders.

OFFICIAL: Mrs Kitchell, you're going to have your seat. You're going to be in London, England in eight hours with little Moe in your arms.

(The BASKETBALL PLAYERS sway and hum.)

You're an LOL and that's something to stand up and be proud of.

WOMAN: Come with us, Mrs Kitchell. It's time to board.

OFFICIAL: It's time.

(MRS KITCHELL jams her knitting needles into bag, more precisely into the gift-wrapped parcel on top. Leaving her bag on the floor, she is hoisted up by the BASKETBALL PLAYERS and carried out in a procession style. An airport CLEANER enters with a push-broom and crosses the stage, turning and recrossing. He pauses when approaching MRS KITCHELL's knitting bag. He listens, and the audience can hear a ticking sound getting louder and louder. He touches the bag and peers in. The ticking gets very loud. He removes the parcel, unwraps the coffeepot, and takes off the lid. A music box begins to play, replacing the ticking, a merry tune that gets louder and louder as the airport CLEANER stares at it. Darkness; curtain.

End of Act One.)

Act Two

(At rise, the same setting—some time in the vague future. The stage is empty except for the luggage platform going slowly around, still carrying the green, pink and silver case. A young airport CLEANER crosses with push-broom, then recrosses. He encounters a LADY on her hands and knees advancing across the stage, running her hand across the floor as though looking for something.)

CLEANER: Excuse me. You lost something, lady?

LADY: What d'ya think?

CLEANER: If it's your contact lenses, give up. People all the time lose their contact lenses, but no one ever finds a contact lens, that's a fact. You ever hear anyone say, "Hey, I've found this contact lens—"?

LADY: It's not my contact lens. My contact lenses are here.

(She points to her eyes.)

CLEANER: Earrings then? Let me tell you, it's a lost cause. Someone finds a earring, they put it in their pocket. Especially if it's gold. People aren't crazy.

LADY: I don't wear earrings. I don't believe in earrings. Earrings are not a part of my belief system.

CLEANER: You lost a dime or something? Then, listen, it's not worth it, crawling around this dirty floor for a dime. Hey, let me give you a dime, what the hell.

LADY: You think I care about money?

CLEANER: Hey! I get it. What you've lost. It's something metaphysical.

LADY: What d'ya know! How'd you guess?

CLEANER: I work in an airport. You know what an airport is? *(Mimicking the voice of "Dragnet's" Joe Friday, he quotes from the radio show "Grand Central Station.")* "It's the crossroads of a million private lives; gigantic stage on which are played a thousand dramas daily."

LADY: Yeah?

CLEANER: People coming. People going. Departures. Arrivals. Get it? It's an equation of the absurd. Going cancels out coming, see? And that means ... no one's going anywhere.

LADY: Hey!

CLEANER: We're all standing still. Like you and me here. We're power-less.

LADY: What about space travel? What about our astronauts?

CLEANER: Interesting question. The answer is—we've given up on this world. We gave it a few million years, and it didn't work out, so now we have to move on. It's our last chance to express our will.

LADY: That's it. That's what I'm looking for. My will. My freedom not to act.

CLEANER: Give up, lady. You're in the hands of the historical dynamic. You can't do a blessed thing but move along.

LADY: I refuse to believe that.

CLEANER: Don't believe then.

LADY: I don't believe we always have to rush toward some theoretical destination, departing, arriving, going in circles. I can choose—

CLEANER: What?

LADY: I can choose nothing. Stillness. I can just—*(Sits in lotus position.)*—I can just *be.*

CLEANER: Well, that's a real nice thought but sentimental if you don't mind my saying so. Didn't you know that sitting still is boring?

PA: Ladies and gentlemen. This is our last and final and ultimate call for non-travelling passengers, this is our zero-hour call.

CLEANER: Lady, you're going to miss your plane.

LADY: The only plane I recognize *(She strokes the floor.)* is the plane of the inner consciousness.

CLEANER: I wouldn't give you odds on the inner consciousness. It can land you in hot water. See that couple over there? They're sad, real sad. A case in point.

(Lights focus on PILOT and FLIGHT ATTENDANT in the same position as in their previous contretemps. The lighting is perhaps a trifle more lurid, the music more lurid as well.)

PILOT: Oh! Hello.

FLIGHT ATTENDANT: Hello.

PILOT: I suppose I ... I should say ... really should say ... congratulations.

FLIGHT ATTENDANT: You've heard then? My first solo. All alone up there. Just me and the clouds and the great big unforgiving sky.

PILOT: What I can't understand ... someone like you, especially someone—

FLIGHT ATTENDANT: It went beautifully. My supervisor gave me full marks. In three weeks I'll have my exams and then—

PILOT: Then?

FLIGHT ATTENDANT: Maybe ... maybe we could ... you know ... when the time comes ... we could maybe ... celebrate?

PILOT: Celebrate?

FLIGHT ATTENDANT: My treat. Dinner maybe. That Japanese place—

PILOT: I'm ... er ... pretty busy these days.

FLIGHT ATTENDANT: And nights too?

PILOT: I wish things had been ... different.

FLIGHT ATTENDANT: Different? Ah, I see. Well.

PILOT: Well.

(They exit; a number of people cross the stage with suitcases.)

PA: Flight 492 for Los Angeles has been delayed. Passengers are asked [inaudible].

(Passengers with suitcases line up at a desk, perhaps the same one that functioned as the insurance booth in Act One. At end of the line are a YOUNG WOMAN and YOUNG MAN. She carries a backpack; he is wearing a business suit. As they speak, others freeze.)

YOUNG WOMAN: Excuse me?

YOUNG MAN: Me?

YOUNG WOMAN: Is this ... can you tell me ... is this the right line?

YOUNG MAN: I hope so.

YOUNG WOMAN: Long. It's long, isn't it?

YOUNG MAN: I've been standing here five minutes and it hasn't budged.

YOUNG WOMAN: Oh, excuse me. Sorry.

YOUNG MAN: Sorry?

YOUNG WOMAN: I knocked you. With my backpack.

YOUNG MAN: Don't mention it. Never felt a thing.

YOUNG WOMAN: Will you look at this crowd. Wonder if it ever slows down.

YOUNG MAN: Doubt it. I travel a lot and I've hardly ever seen a really quiet airport. I mean *really* quiet.

YOUNG WOMAN: Modern life.

YOUNG MAN: You say something?

YOUNG WOMAN: Modern life. Hustle? Bustle?

PA: Flight 492 for Los Angeles has been delayed and will now depart at 9:05.

YOUNG WOMAN: Oh, no, that's my flight. 9:05. That's two whole hours from now.

YOUNG MAN: You really are early.

YOUNG WOMAN: What about you? Which flight are you?

YOUNG MAN: L.A. Same flight.

YOUNG WOMAN: Oh ... so you're kind of early too.

 (Pause.)

YOUNG MAN: Well, I like to be early.

YOUNG WOMAN: Oh.

YOUNG MAN: I didn't intend to be this early but ... well, my girlfriend, she dropped me off. She had an early appointment at work, so ...

YOUNG WOMAN: Did you see that? That man up there. He just barged in front of that lady there.

YOUNG MAN: You have to wonder at guys like that.

YOUNG WOMAN: "A" types. "A" for aggressive.

YOUNG MAN: "K" for klutz.

YOUNG WOMAN: I don't know, people like that. I did this course last winter. Different personality types, you know? Some people can't help themselves. Basically they're insecure and afraid of the world, but they like to push people around.

YOUNG MAN: I guess my girlfriend's a little like that. Very aggressive. If she were here she'd be up there in front demanding to know why we're late.

YOUNG WOMAN: Could be engine trouble. Or weather.

YOUNG MAN: Uh uh, not with that blue sky. Look through the doors there. It's going to be one great day, not a cloud in sight.

YOUNG WOMAN: Well, just that little one.

YOUNG MAN: Where? Oh, yeah. Well, at least there's no wind.

YOUNG WOMAN: Could be the pilot's sick. There's this South American flu going around.

YOUNG MAN: You're telling me. My girlfriend, has she been sick! Had to take a day off work. That's how I knew she was really sick.

YOUNG WOMAN: You know, I used to want to be a pilot. Isn't that crazy? Talk about being unrealistic.

YOUNG MAN: I don't know. Things are changing. My girlfriend? She's the office manager. Instead of taking dictation, she does the dictating.

YOUNG WOMAN: She's still stuck in an office though.

YOUNG MAN: Exactly! That's exactly the point I was making the other day and—

YOUNG WOMAN: We talk about taking charge and all that, but do we ask ourselves what we really want?

YOUNG MAN: Never. Well, hardly ever. Only, in my case, I think I know, sort of.

YOUNG WOMAN: You know what you want? What? But, hey, I guess I really shouldn't ask. I mean, if it's personal.

PA: Passengers for Flight 492 to Los Angeles are advised that departure time is not 9:05.

YOUNG MAN: No, I don't mind you asking. I believe people should ask questions if there's something they really want to know. Otherwise—

YOUNG WOMAN: So what is it? What do you want?

YOUNG MAN: Well, it's a little hard to describe. But let me ask you this. Have you ever tasted goat's milk?

YOUNG WOMAN: Goat's? Milk?

YOUNG MAN: Or, listen, have you ever eaten goat's cheese? Lots of times in restaurants you get these little chunks of this white cheese in your salad?

YOUNG WOMAN: Oh, yeah, sure, I know.

YOUNG MAN: That's goat cheese. Usually. There's nothing like it. Goat cheese's terrific. Texture, flavour, you name it.

YOUNG WOMAN: So you want to get in the business? The goat cheese business?

YOUNG MAN: There's a future in it. I've shown my girlfriend some market projections, but she's—and you can also make a very nice goat's milk soap. Good for the skin. Excellent for the skin.

YOUNG WOMAN: But doesn't it—?

YOUNG MAN: I know what you're going to say. Doesn't it smell? People always think goats smell. They think of goats and they hold their noses.

YOUNG WOMAN: You mean it's not true? You mean goats smell good?

YOUNG MAN: It's the kind of smell you get used to. You almost get so you like it. And the other thing is that goats have excellent dispositions.

They're independent, proud animals, but they can also be affectionate with human beings.

YOUNG WOMAN: Gee, I didn't realize—

YOUNG MAN: I hate to see any species maligned.

YOUNG WOMAN: That can happen. I happen to know—

YOUNG MAN: I'm not saying the goat business doesn't have problems. Let's just say it presents a small growth industry with varied possibilities.

YOUNG WOMAN: So. You've made up your mind. You're going into the goat business.

YOUNG MAN: Well, no. I doubt it. It's unlikely, all things considered.

PA: Passengers for Kansas City, Flight 91, may now board at Gate 12. Passengers for Kansas City [inaudible].

YOUNG WOMAN: Sorry, I didn't hear what you were saying.

YOUNG MAN: I just said, just because you want to do something doesn't mean it's necessarily going to happen.

YOUNG WOMAN: I know what you mean. Oh, brother, do I ever know what you—

YOUNG MAN: Like things ... things get in ... they get in your way.

YOUNG WOMAN: Let me guess. Your girlfriend doesn't go for goats.

YOUNG MAN: Hey, you're very intuitive.

YOUNG WOMAN: Well, I took this night class last winter—

YOUNG MAN: It's not just goats. It's the lifestyle she can't handle.

YOUNG WOMAN: It would be a major change. But sometimes a major change is what we need. A good hard kick, if you know what I mean. As a matter of fact, the reason I'm going to L.A. is—

YOUNG MAN: She's always lived in a large city—

YOUNG WOMAN: Your girlfriend?

YOUNG MAN: She thinks nature means walking around a park looking at the grass. She thinks flowers come in borders. Borders! That's the way they grow, she thinks, a bunch of little pansies in a row.

YOUNG WOMAN: I always think that—

YOUNG MAN: Concerts, museums, art galleries, she's used to having it all. As a matter of fact, that's where we met, at the art gallery.

YOUNG WOMAN: It's hard to meet people in a big city. I've really—

YOUNG MAN: There was this big exhibition. Modern sculpture. A guide was taking us around, a bunch of us, and there was this woman carved out of stone with a big hole in her body, right in the middle, and the guide said—

YOUNG WOMAN: It was easier to meet people in our parents' day. My folks, believe it or not, met at a bridge party. Imagine meeting someone at a bridge party nowadays—

YOUNG MAN: Anyway, the guide said the hole in her body meant there was a sense of incompletion in all human encounters—

YOUNG WOMAN: My grandparents, they met each other at a prayer meeting, a Wednesday night prayer meeting. Can you imagine, it's Wednesday, say, and someone says to you, "Hey, let's go to a prayer meeting and—"

YOUNG MAN: Then, after the tour was over at the art gallery, she and I went to this little place for coffee—

YOUNG WOMAN: Some people recommend singles bars but—

YOUNG MAN: —and right away we seemed to have a lot in common—

YOUNG WOMAN: And as a matter of fact, one reason I signed up for this evening course last winter was so I might maybe meet—

YOUNG MAN: But now, after six months, I don't know if we have anything in common at all. I mean, I think of that woman with the hole through her stomach and I, well … I start to wonder.

YOUNG WOMAN: I see.

YOUNG MAN: It's like, like I've got a hole, in me, but she doesn't even notice.

YOUNG WOMAN: *(Puzzled.)* Exactly.

YOUNG MAN: Lately we seem to be fighting all the time. Last week she came right out and accused me—I could hardly believe this—of being selfish. I mean, I'm the one—well, that's one reason I thought I'd get away for a week. I saw this seat sale and—

YOUNG WOMAN: So did I. Just couldn't resist. I just had to get away, and well, you know what they say about travelling—sometimes you meet—

YOUNG MAN: Once she threw a plate at me.

YOUNG WOMAN: A plate!

YOUNG MAN: A plate … with butter on it.

YOUNG WOMAN: Violence doesn't solve a thing, but sometimes—

YOUNG MAN: Another time she locked herself in the bathroom and stayed in there—

YOUNG WOMAN: Withdrawal. Common pattern for delaying stress. That's one of the things I learned last winter at this—

YOUNG MAN: I mean, in our relationship, I'm the one who vacuums. Did my father ever vacuum? And not only that—

YOUNG WOMAN: What?

YOUNG MAN: Well, I was going to say, I'm the one who takes the sheets down to the laundromat.

YOUNG WOMAN: That's where I've seen you!

YOUNG MAN: Where?

YOUNG WOMAN: I knew you looked familiar!

YOUNG MAN: Yeah?

YOUNG WOMAN: Saturday mornings? Around ten-thirty? That laundromat at Dover and 24th?

YOUNG MAN: What d'ya know!

YOUNG WOMAN: You're usually using machine number three. Drinking coffee out of a paper cup? Cream. No sugar.

YOUNG MAN: Right!

YOUNG WOMAN: And you're usually buried in a paperback. Last week it was … I think it was—

YOUNG MAN: *The War of the Last Planet.* Now that's a very interesting thing. I never read sci-fi, never touch the stuff, except in the laundromat—

YOUNG WOMAN: I think … yes, I'm sure of it … once I asked you if you had four quarters for a dollar. For the dryer? And you said no.

YOUNG MAN: I did?

YOUNG WOMAN: You didn't even check in your pockets. You didn't even look up from your book. You just said no.

YOUNG MAN: Well, I never carry a lot of change on me.

YOUNG WOMAN: No, it wasn't that.

YOUNG MAN: Maybe—

YOUNG WOMAN: You just didn't want to take the trouble.

YOUNG MAN: Maybe it was some other guy. I don't remember—

YOUNG WOMAN: Of course you don't remember. You know something, your girlfriend's right. She's hit the nail on the head. You're selfish.

YOUNG MAN: Hey, wait a minute. Just a minute ago we were having a great conversation about—

YOUNG WOMAN: Conversation. Is this what you call a conversation? I stand here and listen to you rattle on about your goat's milk and your girlfriend and getting hit on the head by a plate full of butter and what a hero you are because you actually take a couple of sheets down to the—

YOUNG MAN: Hey—

YOUNG WOMAN: What about me? *What about me?*

YOUNG MAN: What?

YOUNG WOMAN: Why don't *you* ask *me* about *me*? Me, me, me. Like maybe why I'm going down to L.A. and what I want out of life and whose sheets I'm washing down at the laundromat every Saturday morning—

YOUNG MAN: But you seemed, I thought—

YOUNG WOMAN: —I was enthralled with every golden word that—

YOUNG MAN: You know what I really thought? I thought, here's one woman who's a damned good listener. My girlfriend, on the other hand ...

YOUNG WOMAN: Please. I don't want to hear about your girlfriend.

YOUNG MAN: Hey, I'm sorry. Listen, I really am.

YOUNG WOMAN: You should be. *You should be.*

YOUNG MAN: If I'd just stopped to think—

YOUNG WOMAN: Forget it.

YOUNG MAN: So tell me, what do you want to do? With your life, I mean.

YOUNG WOMAN: That's my business.

YOUNG MAN: But I really want to know.

YOUNG WOMAN: Too bad. You missed your chance.

YOUNG MAN: Couldn't you ... give me another chance? I mean it. I can't stand it. I want to know. What do you want? Out of life?

YOUNG WOMAN: It won't work now.

YOUNG MAN: Oh, please!

YOUNG WOMAN: I want ... I want to meet ... someone. And it's hard. I ask questions. I draw people out, but—why can't someone, just once, draw *me* out?

YOUNG MAN: There are church groups.

YOUNG WOMAN: People always say that.

YOUNG MAN: Or bridge. Have you tried a bridge club?

YOUNG WOMAN: Be serious.

YOUNG MAN: Singles bars. People say they're shabby but—

YOUNG WOMAN: They *are* shabby.

YOUNG MAN: I know! A night course.

YOUNG WOMAN: I already told you—

YOUNG MAN: Or the art gallery. No, not a good idea, forget it.

YOUNG WOMAN: I thought maybe ... an airport—

YOUNG MAN: An airport? Why an airport?

YOUNG WOMAN: I don't know. People who travel are, well, you know, they're sort of restless.

YOUNG MAN: Restless? Maybe. Could be.

YOUNG WOMAN: They're looking for ... something.

YOUNG MAN: Maybe. You might be—

YOUNG WOMAN: Oh, sorry.

YOUNG MAN: Sorry?

YOUNG WOMAN: I knocked you. With my back-pack. Again.

YOUNG MAN: That's a ... that's a nice backpack. I really like that ... stitching.

YOUNG WOMAN: I don't think this line has budged an inch.

YOUNG MAN: We'll get there eventually.

YOUNG WOMAN: I hope so.

YOUNG MAN: Why don't you ... just to pass the time ... why don't you— tell me about yourself? This course you were taking—

(They are overwhelmed by the noise of the airport. A WOMAN TELEPHONER enters, goes to phone booth and dials.)

WOMAN TELEPHONER: *(Affecting a French accent.) Allo?* Is this Mrs. Harrow? Please may I speak with Mister Harrow? It is a business affair, *oui? (She switches to her regular voice.)* Josh! It's me. Ta da! I'm out at the airport. I know, I know, but I was hoping *you'd* answer, damn it. Anyway, I told her it was a business affair. Ha! Besides, I was curious, just a little bit curious. Well, just to see what her voice was like. No, I thought she sounded very ... soft. Nice. Friendly, sort of. Sweet, in fact, damn it.

Josh, look, I'm just between planes kind of thing. Edmonton. Oh, the usual thing, we're setting up a new show, more grain elevators against the fading sun. It's a bottomless market, I'm happy to say. Anyway, what I want to know is—is there any chance you could get to Edmonton for a couple of days? I'm not going to be all that busy once the show's installed, and we could ... What? I didn't think so. I guess this means you haven't told her yet. No, I know. Well, you did say that as soon as she got her root canal work done. You did say that. So how far along is she now? I see. Four more on the bottom. She didn't sound like she was in pain. No, I know it's serious. No, I'm not making light of it. Oh. Oh! Well, not exactly. What does that involve? Well, I can't help it, I never knew anyone who had a jaw realignment. Is she thinking about it, or ...? It's definite then. No, I can see that. But after they take the wires out— yes, it certainly does sound major. Uh huh. No, you're right, you couldn't do that. I agree, only an out-and-out bastard would—no, I'm serious. I'm not being cynical. Teeth are teeth. We've got to hang on to our teeth, we've got to hang on to something in this rotten life.

(She hangs up and exits. A man, RICHARD, and woman, FRANNIE, rush in from opposite sides, carrying luggage. They nearly collide.)

RICHARD: Can you tell me which gate the plane for Toronto leaves from?

FRANNIE: Pardon?

RICHARD: For God's sake! Frannie!

FRANNIE: Christ, I don't believe this. You know something, Richard?— you look like you've seen a ghost.

RICHARD: So do you. You look … stunned.

FRANNIE: It's just … I mean, this is the last place I expected to see you.

RICHARD: How long's it been? Eight years? Since the divorce, I mean.

FRANNIE: Let's see—it was 1981 when you went through that door—

RICHARD: *(Wistfully.)* God, that long!

FRANNIE: *(Nostalgically.)* Yeah.

RICHARD: So how've you been? How you been doing?

FRANNIE: Not bad, not bad at all.

RICHARD: You're looking great. I mean it. Great.

FRANNIE: Really?

RICHARD: Really.

FRANNIE: So are you. Your hair—

RICHARD: Getting a little grey—

FRANNIE: It suits you. You know, it really does, really.

RICHARD: Well, well.

FRANNIE: *(After a brief silence.)* Well. So you're off to Toronto?

RICHARD: Just changing planes. I usually get the direct flight, but the goddamn air strike—

FRANNIE: *(Deeply sympathetic.)* I know.

RICHARD: You off to Toronto too?

FRANNIE: The west coast.

RICHARD: The west coast?

FRANNIE: I live there now.

RICHARD: Well, what d'ya know. Lotus land. I heard you'd married again.

FRANNIE: I can't get over how terrific you look.

RICHARD: A lawyer or something like that. Someone I ran into, Reg, I think, told me you and some big shot lawyer were—

FRANNIE: Reg? You mean Reg Barnstable?

RICHARD: I run into Reg the odd time at the annual do.

FRANNIE: How is he anyway? Old Reg?

RICHARD: Not bad. Looking a little older but—

FRANNIE: —but who isn't?

RICHARD: And he told me you were seeing this guy, some lawyer—

FRANNIE: Now how would Reg Barnstable know a thing like that?

RICHARD: Well, you know Reg.

FRANNIE: Always had a nose for the latest dirt. Always poking his nose in—

RICHARD: Reg was saying it looked like wedding bells—you and this lawyer.

FRANNIE: Hmmm.

RICHARD: Well, for God's sake, Frannie, was it wedding bells? I mean, is it?

FRANNIE: It didn't work out.

RICHARD: Oh.

FRANNIE: Same old problem.

RICHARD: Oh?

FRANNIE: The old career me versus the old dependent me.

RICHARD: Oh, yeah.

FRANNIE: How about you? Still enjoying your ... your ... freedom? Or—?

RICHARD: Same old freedom!

FRANNIE: Do what you want—

RICHARD: —when you want—

FRANNIE: —with whomever you want—

RICHARD: Finding that great lotus land of the inner self.

FRANNIE: Right on.

RICHARD: What is lotus, anyway? I mean, what the hell is it?

FRANNIE: Hmmm. I'm not sure. Something Greek, anyway. Some kind of fruit maybe?

RICHARD: Something from mythology. We had it in school, I think.

FRANNIE: They're leaves. I just remembered. Lotus leaves.

RICHARD: Like spinach, you mean?

FRANNIE: No, they're from trees, I think. It's all coming back.

RICHARD: From trees? You sure?

FRANNIE: Just a min. I'll check.

(She sits down on her suitcase, rummages in her tote bag, pulls out a large dog-eared book, and turns over the pages as RICHARD listens.)

Hmmm, "see jujube." *(Turning pages.)* "Any tree or shrub of the buckthorn family," hmmm. Richard? Are you listening?

RICHARD: All ears.

FRANNIE: You look like you're in some kind of trance. *(She snaps her fingers.)* What's with it with you?

RICHARD: I was just thinking how you haven't changed a bit.

FRANNIE: Oh, I've changed. I'm a lotus-eater now, remember. So are you. I've … we've arrived.

RICHARD: But listen, you've still got your wonderful goddamn book. You still look up every god-damn thing.

FRANNIE: Well, of course, how else are you going to know anything?

RICHARD: I used to say, "Let's make love," and you'd pull out your book and you'd look it up in the index and you'd say, "Now, there are eight basic positions and twenty-six comfortable variations."

FRANNIE: Twenty-six? You sure? *(Turning pages.)* I think you're a little low there.

RICHARD: It was just an example.

FRANNIE: An example of what?

RICHARD: Of the way you were. Oh, you were lovely, you know.

FRANNIE: Do you know what you said to me once, Richard? It was the nicest thing you ever said to me.

RICHARD: What? Tell me.

FRANNIE: I don't think I want to now.

RICHARD: Why not? I said it, for God's sake. I have a right—

FRANNIE: It would spoil it, the memory. If I said it out loud. Especially in a … an airport.

RICHARD: But I must have said it out loud.

FRANNIE: There are some things you can only say once. Otherwise they get spoiled. You might turn around and say it to someone else.

RICHARD: Tell me. Please.

(FRANNIE puts her mouth up to his ear; there is a sound of a plane in background.)

RICHARD: Can't hear you.

FRANNIE: I said—

(She is drowned out by the sound of three people rushing by with suitcases.)

RICHARD: Once more.

FRANNIE: I said. You said ... you said, "Your body is like a bouquet of flowers."

RICHARD: I can't believe I said that. "Your body is like a bouquet of flowers."

FRANNIE: You said it all right. I can tell you exactly where and when it was if you like. *(She fishes in her bag for another book.)* Here we go. My diary. Lake Louise. 1978. July second. Remember? We went for that long weekend.

RICHARD: Jesus, yes. That little cabin by the lake.

FRANNIE: Those crazy racoons.

(They both laugh uproariously.)

RICHARD: And those goddamn cute squirrels. *(Laughs.)*

FRANNIE: *(Choking with laughter.)* And you fed them— *(Laughs.)*— remember? You fed them ... bread.

(They both explode with laughter.)

RICHARD: *(Suddenly.)* I loved the backs of your knees.

FRANNIE: Pardon?

RICHARD: The backs of your knees. I loved that particular part of your body, those little pink creases—

FRANNIE: Richard, for Pete's sake—

RICHARD: I used to nuzzle the backs of your knees. You'd be lying on the bed reading one of your goddamn books and I'd nuzzle and nuzzle and nuzzle and nuzzle—

FRANNIE: Really? I wonder why. There, I mean.

RICHARD: Because you had beautiful backs to your knees, that's why.

FRANNIE: *(Turning and trying to look.)* Did I really?

RICHARD: Yes. You did. And you probably still do. Some things don't change.

FRANNIE: *(She tries again to see.)* I can't quite—

RICHARD: Frannie, you know what I'd like?

FRANNIE: You'd like what?

RICHARD: Well, I haven't any right to ask this but—

FRANNIE: Go ahead.

RICHARD: I'd give a hell of a lot, Frannie, just to see the backs of your knees again.

FRANNIE: I thought you had a plane to catch.

RICHARD: I've got a couple of minutes. Look, Frannie, you could bend over and put your book back, and I could stoop down and pretend to tie my shoe at the same time—

FRANNIE: You sure this isn't a bit—perverted?

RICHARD: Frannie, oh Frannie. Just a quick look.

FRANNIE: Well, just a quick one. Are you ready?

RICHARD: One, two, three, go!

(In an orchestrated movement he stoops to tie shoe; she bends over her bag. There is a drum roll, a clash of cymbals. She and he rise together, breathless.)

Oh, Frannie!

(A man, ONLOOKER, approaches from the side.)

ONLOOKER: Wait a minute. I've been watching you. Knees! Nuzzling!

FRANNIE: And who the hell are you?

ONLOOKER: I'm an onlooker. Just minding my business. Doing my job.

RICHARD: Seems to me you're minding our business.

FRANNIE: Butting in.

ONLOOKER: Onlookers have rights too. Here's my card. "Onlookers, Bystanders and Passers-by." And some of us have come out against drum rolls in public airports.

RICHARD: I can't be responsible for—

ONLOOKER: There are rules, you know, for estranged couples who meet accidentally—

FRANNIE: I happen to have my book of rules with me. *(She rummages in her sack.)* Now let me see—

RICHARD: Hey, wait a minute—

ONLOOKER: A calm handshake is usually recommended in cases—

FRANNIE: Hey, you're not just a random onlooker. I know who you are. You're—

RICHARD: Reg Barnstable!

FRANNIE: You old dirt-shoveller, you! *(She embraces him.)*

RICHARD: My favourite old rumour-monger, how the hell are you?

(The three of them exit with arms around each other, talking inaudibly; lights go on, spotting PILOT and FLIGHT ATTENDANT in the fourth contretemps.)

FLIGHT ATTENDANT: You sent for me.

PILOT: I did.

FLIGHT ATTENDANT: Well, here I am, Sir.

PILOT: So I see.

FLIGHT ATTENDANT: Reporting for duty. Sir?

PILOT: You realize you have been assigned with me on the new northwest flight.

FLIGHT ATTENDANT: I do.

PILOT: You know my feelings about—

FLIGHT ATTENDANT: —women in the cockpit? Yes, I do, Sir. I could apply for a transfer, Sir.

PILOT: *(Shifting tone.)* How can you call me Sir ... after what we've meant to each other ... that night at the Japanese rest—

FLIGHT ATTENDANT: I won't forget how you struggled ... first with the sushi ... then with the chopsticks ... how hard you tried—persevering—

PILOT: It's not easy ... not easy at all, for a man, a man like me ... to change ... to admit he might be wrong.

FLIGHT ATTENDANT: Are you saying what I think you're saying? What I hope you're saying?

PILOT: I'm not saying that ... only that ... times change, we all have to—

(They embrace; lights fade. A young man, CALLER, approaches the phone booth and dials.)

CALLER: Sherry Hutchuk, please. Sherry? Hey, it's great to hear your voice. Bet you can't guess who this is. No. No. Hey, wait a minute. Don't hang up. I'll give you a big hint. Quebec City. 1987. No, June. After the rock concert? Yeah. That's right. No, that was Arnie. I was the one with the CCM. Now you've got it. Yeah. Were we wiped! Yeah, well I remember part of it. Anyway, I'm on my way to Seattle. I gotta promise of a job out there, kind of important, and we had a stop here, so I pull out my book and there you are. Yeah, I'm out at the airport. No, I'm standing right here, no shit. Why should I lie?

(Lights go up on PILOT and FLIGHT ATTENDANT; soap-opera music.)

PILOT: If only you'd told me. How you felt. I didn't ... now I see what you—

FLIGHT ATTENDANT: I didn't want ... to hurt you. I tried. You tried. We both tried. But.

(Lights fade; spotlight on the phone booth.)

CALLER: What d'ya mean, why? I don't have *anything* on my mind. The stewardess just said we could get off for twenty-five fast ones and stretch our legs and put in a call, so I thought, who do I know here? and then I thought of you and that terrific night in Kee-bec and—you've got to go right now? You mean this minute? Why can't you go to the dry-cleaners in twenty-five minutes? Oh. Well, if that's the way it is. Well, tell me quick then, how've you been? Oh. Oh? What d'ya know.

(Light fades and comes up on PILOT and FLIGHT ATTENDANT; soap-opera music.)

PILOT: I understand.

FLIGHT ATTENDANT: No, I understand.

PILOT: We both understand. That's what's so—

FLIGHT ATTENDANT: Yes, yes, yes, yes, yes.

(Light snaps off and comes up on phone booth.)

CALLER: Well. Well. Well, I guess I oughta say congrats. So when's the big day? Yeah? That right? Hey, you still there? Well, you said you had to go to the dry-cleaners so I thought … Listen, that night in Quebec City, I wasn't all that skunked, you know. I remember quite a lot, in fact. And I bet you do too. Remember we were up there at the what-do-you-call-it, that place where you look down and see all the lights, and we got to talking and you told me about how your cat got killed and you started to cry and, Jesus, so did I almost, and yeah, yeah, well, I remember things like that. I really remember that whole night. The stars and the moon and all that. That wet grass and those little, little bugs. I thought, this girl's special. I was hoping maybe, wishing you maybe, well, yeah, I know, you gotta go to the dry-cleaners, so well, all the best. *(Hangs up phone and an instant later kicks side of phone booth.)* Bitch!

(People cross and recross the stage with luggage. An elderly man, WESLEY, and an elderly woman, MYRA, are left standing by the luggage platform which is revolving with MYRA's suitcase on it. WESLEY grabs for it, but misses.)

MYRA: That's mine, I believe.

WESLEY: Thought it might be.

(He grabs again, successfully.)

MYRA: You must be Wesley.

WESLEY: That's right. I am.

MYRA: Well, I'm Myra.

WESLEY: Pleased to meet you. *(Gesturing to the suitcase.)* Heavy.

MYRA: *(Injured.)* Heavy?

WESLEY: But not too heavy. You expect a suitcase to be heavy. This is almost … almost … light.

MYRA: You said you'd be wearing a fur-trimmed overcoat. That's how I knew you.

WESLEY: Well, it's not much of an overcoat. I shouldn't have worn it, but I said I would. The lining's getting worn and I only wore it because—

MYRA: It looks just fine to me. Serviceable. For the climate, I mean. It's a waste of money going along with the fashion every time some so-called designer down in New York City decides that now it's time for wide shoulders or narrow shoulders or—

WESLEY: That's what I think—

MYRA: So what if it's a little worn? If it's good quality to start with—and I can tell this is one hundred percent wool—where are you going to find that these days? You get nothing but synthetics or blends, though I do say some of these blends are marvellous in their way. *(Pause.)* For wrinkles.

WESLEY: Yes, that's true. *(Pause.)* For wrinkles.

MYRA: A little altering can do wonders with a good basic overcoat with—

PA: Flight 756 for Detroit, Pittsburgh, and Philadelphia now boarding.

MYRA: Wesley, I'm going to get right back on that plane and go back to New Brunswick.

WESLEY: But—

MYRA: I should never have come. My sister Ruth—I wrote you about her—she said it would never work out, two people with nothing in common.

WESLEY: But you just got here.

MYRA: We've just met and all we've talked about is your old overcoat. You'll think that's all I ever talk about. Just rattling on and on. That's not true. I don't usually go on this way. Now, I'm not going to say another word. I'm going to give you a chance to talk.

WESLEY: I'm not a great one for talking. I think that's why—

MYRA: —why you haven't met anyone—

WESLEY: —since my wife—

MYRA: —died.

WESLEY: Now, she was a talker.

MYRA: Not my husband. He was a quiet man. Kept to himself. But up here … *(She taps her forehead.)* there was plenty going on.

WESLEY: Oh.

MYRA: Only thing, I never knew what it was.

WESLEY: I guess I'm a little like that.

MYRA: Well, still waters—

WESLEY: —run deep.

MYRA: My mother used to say that. She was full of sayings. The stories she could tell. Lots of people at home think I take after her.

PA: Last call for Detroit, Pittsburgh, and Philadelphia.

MYRA: I shouldn't have come. This is ... ridiculous. I see what Ruth meant when she—

WESLEY: You're tired, all that distance—

MYRA: I didn't tell Ruth you paid for my ticket. She wouldn't have thought it was right. It isn't right.

WESLEY: But I wanted—

MYRA: Now I'm really and truly not going to say one more word. I swear. I'm going to give you a chance to talk.

(A long pause.)

WESLEY: I don't know how to begin. What topic, I mean.

MYRA: *(Through closed lips.)* I'm not going to say another word.

(Very long pause.)

WESLEY: That's a pretty coat you're wearing.

MYRA: *(Through closed lips.)* Thank you.

WESLEY: I like that shade of ... well, whatever it is ... purple.

MYRA: *(Through closed lips.)* Burgundy.

WESLEY: What was that?

MYRA: *(Through closed lips.)* Burgundy. *(She opens her mouth.)* Burgundy.

WESLEY: Oh.

MYRA: My favourite colour.

(Another long pause.)

WESLEY: It gets pretty cold here.

(Silence.)

You need a good warm coat like that ... here.

MYRA: Go on. You're doing fine.

WESLEY: Take right now. Coldest winter since 1952. Said so in the paper the other night.

MYRA: Did it now? This is fascinating.

WESLEY: Of course you can't always believe the paper. Last fall they predicted a drought.

MYRA: And what happened? What happened, Wesley?

WESLEY: Rain.

MYRA: There, you see. You can't believe the papers. So there was rain, was there? How much rain?

WESLEY: Lots of rain. Of course, I don't mind the rain.

MYRA: I like to walk in the rain. Of course I take my umbrella and galoshes.

WESLEY: That's what caught my eye.

MYRA: How do you mean, Wesley? Caught your eye?

WESLEY: In the ad.

MYRA: Oh, that ad! I don't know what got into me.

WESLEY: It was the part where it said, "Likes long walks. And gardening."

MYRA: Ruth said I was out of my mind. She said some pervert would be writing back and answering that ad.

WESLEY: I almost didn't. *(Pause.)* Write, I mean.

MYRA: But one morning I was out walking. I do a mile and a half every day.

WESLEY: That's what struck me. A mile and a half. Now, I do three kilometres and that's just about, give or take a few yards, just about—

MYRA: I was going along this old road that leads out of town, pretty road, lots of elms, though the elms are pretty well gone—

WESLEY: It's starting here too. The elms. It breaks your—

MYRA: —and I was going around this curve where the gas station is and the Bowie farm and then there's this straight stretch and I could see straight ahead for miles and miles, just straight ahead and ... and there wasn't anything there.

WESLEY: It's like that here. You can see for miles and—

MYRA: Nothing at all. I don't know why, but it scared me to death. My teeth started to chatter, does that ever happen to you? It was just miles and miles and I could tell that if I walked along there, nothing was going to happen to me. I was just going to keep on walking, and then I got so hot and I started to ... well ... I started to cry, now isn't that the craziest thing you ever heard?

WESLEY: I like a good long walk.

MYRA: Well, I just decided right there on the spot that I'd put an ad in the *Rose Lovers' Quarterly*, even if it was a crazy thing to do, and like Ruth said, dangerous maybe, but I said to myself, now would a sex pervert be reading the *Rose Lovers' Quarterly*? Well, yes and no, I thought, you can never tell, but your letter came along—it was the only one, you know—and I knew right away that I didn't have to worry. But that's not true, I did worry. I worried all the way here—

WESLEY: It's only normal. To worry.

MYRA: And I've got the return ticket. It's good up till six months.

WESLEY: That'll be lots of time. To get acquainted, I mean. And you'll see my roses when they come out.

MYRA: That's right!

WESLEY: Lots of people in this climate give up on roses. It's getting them through the winter's the problem. I have these windbreaks, and of course, I cover everything in the fall. I use good quality canvas. Sometimes I lost a few. But—

MYRA: —but some of them get through!

WESLEY: They look dead at first. But little by little they come back.

MYRA: It's a challenge.

WESLEY: I forget who said it, but someone once said, "A Manitoba rose is a rose that knows no fear."

MYRA: Knows no fear! I like that.

WESLEY: I've got the spare room all spruced up. It's got a nice big closet. You'll like ... the closet. My wife—

MYRA: Let's make a pact, Wesley. Do you like to be called Wesley or do you like Wes?

WESLEY: Wesley's fine with me. My wife always—

MYRA: Let's make a pact. Let's try not to talk too much about *them.*

WESLEY: Them? You mean—

MYRA: Them. You know. Your wife and—

WESLEY: —and your husband.

MYRA: I have this funny feeling that they're, you know—

WESLEY: —watching us. I know what you mean.

MYRA: Yes. Looking down at us and saying, aren't they the sillies!

WESLEY: And at their age! You should hear my son and his wife Darlene. They think I've gone senile. They wonder what the neighbours will think ... about the spare room being all spruced up and all.

MYRA: Maybe we are senile. Have you thought of that?

WESLEY: Darlene says to me, "Well, I suppose you need the companionship."

MYRA: Everyone's always talkin' about companionship. Funny word that. Like companionship's all you're up to.

WESLEY: My wife—

MYRA: We weren't going to—

WESLEY: Just this once. My wife was ... not very well ... almost an invalid ... for a long time. But ... *(He clears his throat.)* I'm in quite good health, excellent health.

MYRA: My husband, well, we were different. He wasn't all that, you know, demonstrative. But I was ... always ... demonstrative. That's the way I was made, I can't help it.

WESLEY: The spare room I've fixed up? If you don't feel comfortable there you could always—it does have a good closet though.

MYRA: I don't have a lot of clothes. Just a few things, my walking shoes—

WESLEY: Good—

MYRA: And a few rose cuttings—

WESLEY: Cuttings!

MYRA: Just the hardier varieties, of course. And my garden tools. A person gets used to her own ... trowel.

WESLEY: That's true. A person gets used to things.

MYRA: But a person can change. Adapt.

WESLEY: New growth.

MYRA: I like the way you put that, new growth. You're a very attractive man, Wesley. I'd say that snap you sent doesn't do you justice.

WESLEY: You're a little different than I thought too. More filled out and happy looking.

MYRA: Shall we go? You sure that isn't too heavy?

WESLEY: Light as a feather. A feather!

(They exit. An ELDERLY MAN and ELDERLY WOMAN are standing about halfway up the stairs. Lighting suggests their ethereal quality, and their voices have a degree of echo. They glide up the stairs together, in step, and stand facing audience.)

ELDERLY MAN: Did you hear that?

ELDERLY WOMAN: I certainly did.

ELDERLY MAN: Not too demonstrative, she says. Fine way for a woman to talk about her deceased spouse.

ELDERLY WOMAN: What about the part about the wife being an invalid?

ELDERLY MAN: I wondered about that.

ELDERLY WOMAN: Ever hear of an allergy to roses?

ELDERLY MAN: Never cared for roses myself. Too floppy.

ELDERLY WOMAN: Six months and she'll have her fill.

ELDERLY MAN: She'll talk his ears off, poor fellow.

ELDERLY WOMAN: He'll be dragging her to bulb shows and what not.

ELDERLY MAN: Tramping around the countryside.

ELDERLY WOMAN: Muddy boots.

ELDERLY MAN: What gets into folks?

ELDERLY WOMAN: Foolishness.

ELDERLY MAN: Well, shall we be getting on our way?

> *(They link arms and glide away. A MOTHER, smartly dressed, enters holding two children by the hand, BOY and GIRL, who are adults dressed as children. She speaks in a loud stagey voice as though reading a script.)*

MOTHER: Well, children, isn't this nice! Daddy's coming home. His plane will be in in five minutes.

BOY and GIRL: Yippee.

MOTHER: Now behave yourselves. And stop that, Sammy. You're getting your knees dirty. What will Daddy think?

BOY: *(Mocking.)* What will Daddy think?

MOTHER: *(As though reading lines.)* What *will* Daddy think?

BOY: Who cares what the old barf thinks?

MOTHER: Now don't be a Mister Smartypants. Your Daddy's been on that plane all afternoon—

GIRL: He's always riding on planes, lucky suck.

MOTHER: I think he's coming now. Yes, there he is.

> *(FATHER comes down the "Arrivals" stairs, pecks MOTHER on the cheek, pats the BOY on the head, and twigs the GIRL's ear, then the four of them step back and appraise each other.)*

MOTHER: We never do it right, never. Other families can do it, but not us.

FATHER: What is it? Is it that we lack style? Panache?

BOY: We're boring.

GIRL: We're scared to rip loose.

MOTHER: *(Glancing at her watch.)* What do you say if … if we try it again?

> *(The family resumes their former positions of waiting for FATHER's arrival. This is not a "real" filming, but an extension of the characters' self-consciousness as they indulge in the self-conscious drama of an airport reunion. A DIRECTOR and an ASSISTANT DIRECTOR enter from the side dressed in white, carrying rope for partitions. They also carry white chairs, a white clapperboard, and a knitting bag.)*

DIRECTOR: Ready for the retake, everyone? Now look, guys, a little more … warmth?

ASSISTANT DIRECTOR: *(With a clapperboard.)* One, two, three—roll.

MOTHER: *(Enthusiastically.)* Just five more minutes, kids.

GIRL: Whee! Daddy's going to be here in five minutes.

DIRECTOR: Wait a minute. I think what I'd like is to see you two kids jumping up and down.

BOY: What for?

DIRECTOR: Excitement. You're dying to see your old man. He's been away a whole week. And you, Mom, I want you carrying a knitting bag, okay? And can you loosen that coat a bit—great!

ASSISTANT DIRECTOR: *(Giving MOTHER a knitting bag, using clapperboard.)* One, two, three, roll 'em.

BOY: *(Jumping up and down.)* Five whole minutes, I can't wait.

GIRL: *(Jumping and puffing.)* I ... can't ... wait either.

MOTHER: *(Waving her bag.)* There he is!

> *(FATHER enters, descends, picks up the GIRL, embraces MOTHER, and chucks the BOY under the chin.)*

DIRECTOR: Okay, hold everything. We still don't have it. Let's have some urgency. You, Dad, when you come down those stairs, I want you to give the crowd a ... you know, a searching look. You're home, man, this is your own little nuclear unit. And I want one of you kids to duck under the rope when you see your old man coming.

> *(The DIRECTOR strings a rope across the "Arrivals" and "Departures" stairs.)*

BOY: I will. I'll duck under the rope.

GIRL: What about me? I wanna—

ASSISTANT DIRECTOR: *(As though struck by creative thunder.)* What would happen, I wonder, if they both slipped under the ropes?

DIRECTOR: I could go with that.

ASSISTANT DIRECTOR: Could be a nice touch. Kids released from maternal control for an instant, passion over reason kind of thing—

DIRECTOR: Okay, roll it. Oh, and you, Mama, let's see a look of longing on your face. Your mate's been gone for a whole week and—

MOTHER: How's that?

DIRECTOR: Let's get rid of the gloves, eh. Okay.

ASSISTANT DIRECTOR: One, two, three—action!

BOY: *(Jumping.)* Oh boy, oh boy, five more minutes!

GIRL: *(Jumping.)* Five minutes, four minutes, three minutes—

MOTHER: *(Jumping.)* A whole week!

BOY: There he is. *(He slips under the rope.)*

GIRL: Wait for me. *(She slips under the rope.)*

MOTHER: *(Hitching up her dress and stepping over the rope.)* At last, darling.

DIRECTOR: Not bad. Night and day, in fact. One more take and we'll have it. I want you to show me your pain this time. You, Pops, get a piece of rope around that briefcase of yours ... frayed rope. Now you've got it.

ASSISTANT DIRECTOR: Hey, what if we put the father in a wheelchair?

DIRECTOR: I dunno. It's a possibility—hey! Crutches.

ASSISTANT DIRECTOR: I could go with crutches.

DIRECTOR: Listen, Pops, I want you to kiss the boy. It's okay, it goes nowadays. That's the idea. Then you press the kids' heads to your belly—right, right, heads to belly—and sort of shut your eyes and look upwards—terrific!

ASSISTANT DIRECTOR: Take your places, one, two, three.

BOY: *(Half-crazed.)* Five more minutes!

MOTHER: *Mon dieu*, there he is, thank the dear Lord.

CHILDREN: Papa, Papa!

DIRECTOR: Okay, okay, focus on the kids, get the runny nose, good, great, go for it, show me what you're feeling, go for it.

(FATHER enters, searches the crowd with madman's eyes, runs and embraces his wildly heaving wife and hysterical children.)

DIRECTOR: Hold it an extra second. Can you shudder just a bit more? God, it's fantastic, I love it, the moisture is—okay, break. *(To the ASSISTANT DIRECTOR.)* What d'ya think?

ASSISTANT DIRECTOR: We've got it. Congrats, folks.

(He removes the rope.)

MOTHER: I knew we could do it.

PA: Ladies and gentlemen, will you kindly board.

(The six actors freeze. They listen to announcement, but don't know what to make of it. The announcement is repeated, growing more and more severe.)

Ladies and gentlemen, it is time to board. Now. This minute. Last call. Final call. Departure time has arrived and that means now!

(While the PA makes the announcement, five actors arrange themselves in the shape of an airplane; the two people in front simulate the sound of jets; the two people in the middle hold out arms to suggest wings and wing flaps; the last person forms the tail section. They go through the motions of take-off. Overlapping voices form the sound of the motors.)

VOICES: woe woe woe woe woe
man man man man man man man man
wo man wo man wo man wo man wo man
chow chow chow chow chow chow
ow ow ow ow ow ow ow ow

> *(FLIGHT ATTENDANT stands to one side of the other actors, and as she speaks in sweet tones her arms follow the stylized movements which air personnel use while demonstrating safety procedures—she continues to do this throughout her speech, even though the gestures and words have nothing to connect them.)*

FLIGHT ATTENDANT: Ladies and gentlemen, *mesdames et messieurs,* we hope you have a pleasant flight today. Our flight attendants will soon be serving a light lunch followed by *gateau cerise*—that's cherry cake— and a selection of drinks. Weather conditions are excellent and below you you can see vast fields of corn, wheat and other interesting grain crops. The clouds to your left are of the cumulus variety and typical of the region. You are invited to take photographs if you so wish. Aircraft personnel can assist you with manicures or small psychological crises. If you wish counselling, please put on your light and wait patiently and pleasantly. Or you may wish to join one of our in-flight clubs. We have stamp collecting in the forward section, crochet work in the rear and, conditions permitting, aerobic dancing in the aisle.

> *(She stops talking abruptly, as though a record has been switched off in her head, tiptoes to edge of stage, and looks down as though from a great height. Her tone becomes lyrical, a tone which is both a satire of cheap lyricism and a celebration of transcendence.)*

Oh, look at that, just look at that. Did you ever ... I can never get over it. I look down and suddenly this plane seems to turn transparent and I feel I'm made out of glass and I'm part of the sky and the clouds ... and, oh my God, I look down and there it is, our own little green planet spinning and spinning and spinning with its own sweet crazy unsingable music and—

> *(She looks up dazed; rises; goes back to her official voice.)*

Ladies and gentlemen, *mesdames et messieurs*, we are about to descend. Will you kindly lean to the left. Will the gentleman who is not leaning to the left please do so at this time. We ask that you remove your shoes for landing—we are about to land and require your co-operation in this matter. Lean left. Thank you. *Merci.* Left again. I see one of our lady passengers has not removed her designer boots at this time. May we ask for full cooperation for a smooth and cheerful landing. A little to the left again. For additional oxygen open mouth as wide as possible and please lean forward at this time and commence with foot action. Left, right, left, *mesdames et messieurs*, *gauche, gauche*, left for God's sake, left!

(Actors forming the plane shuffle-step off stage. A minor tinkling crash, more musical than otherwise—similar to the music box that ended Act One—is heard from the wings.)

We hope you have enjoyed your flight with us today and I wish you all a pleasant evening. I wish you a splendid evening, a perfect evening. I wish you a night from which the clouds of pessimism have vanished and a quality of rare moonlight that—

(Music; everyone sweeps in. PILOT takes the FLIGHT ATTENDANT's arm. Music swells, not quite a wedding march but a suggestion of one. The PILOT crowns the "bride" with ribbons and flowers suggesting reconciliation. They ascend steps; others follow hurling confetti. At the top of the stairs the bridal pair turns, faces each other, salutes, and then embraces. They exit and others follow, throwing confetti and taking pictures. The airport CLEANER enters with a push-broom, pauses at centre stage and addresses the audience. Lights dim.)

CLEANER: *(In sincere tones.)* Very few people realize that in the busy life of a major airport there are moments of silence. Generally it's about two or three in the morning. Like right now. Listen. The noise of the giant jets is stilled. Their great silver bodies are at rest, the thunder of their engines silent. At this hour one senses a deep calm rising out of the absence of commerce and the petty distractions of human activity. For this brief interval:

The people of the sky are at peace;
Their frantic comings and goings have ceased
At this hour *(Pause.)* the airport *(Pause.)* sleeps.

(These last three lines should have the feeling of an epilogue, the rhyme stressed, a sense of winding down. The CLEANER exits; lights grow very dim. At the same instant a tiny FAIRY appears spotlighted at the top of the "Arrivals" stairs. She is carrying a lit wand. She dances lightly down the stairs in a dainty ballet step, pauses, surveys the dark and empty airport, spies the silver bag rotating on the luggage platform, takes it, then points her wand at the automatic doors which open to the sound of tinkling music. She exits.

The end.)